D1310569

Tony Gwynn

He Left His Heart in San Diego

by Rich Wolfe

Published by Lone Wolfe Press, a division of Richcraft. Distribution, marketing, publicity, interviews, and book signings handled by Wolfegang Marketing Systems, Ltd.—But Not Very.

This book is not affiliated with or endorsed by the San Diego Padres or MLB.

Photo Credits:
> Front Cover Image: Tim Mantoani
> Inside back flap: Doug Melvold
> K.C. Alfred/UT San Diego via Getty Images, 114, 175, 179, 180, 189,
> K.C. Alfred/UT San Diego, 173, 176, 185, 186
> Jim Baird/ UT San Diego, 177, 181, 184, 192
> Don Bartlett/UT San Diego, 161
> Nelvin Cepeda/UT San Diego, 188
> Robert Gauthier/UT San Diego, 165, 166
> Russ Gilbert / UT San Diego, 163
> Sean M Haffey, 168, 174, 183, 187, 200
> Don Kohlbauer, 169
> John McCutchen/UT San Diego, 167
> Frank McGrath, 191
> Hayne Palmour IV/UT San Diego, 172, 182, 190, 199
> Jerry Rife/UT San Diego, 168
> George Smith, 162
>
> Photos on pages 170, 171, 178 used with permission by Louisville Slugger Museum & Factory®

Layout: The Printed Page, Phoenix, AZ
Author's agent: T. Roy Gaul

Rich Wolfe can be reached at 602-738-5889

ISBN: 978-0-9846278-9-9

> ***PAGE TWO.** In 1941, the news director at a small radio station in Kalamazoo, Michigan hired Harry Caray who had been employed at a station in Joliet, Illinois. The news director's name was Paul Harvey. Yes, that PAUL HARVEY! "And now, you have the rest of the story...

DEDICATION

John Hrycko

the hardest working and nicest man alive

ACKNOWLEDGMENTS

The giant tip of the Hatlo hat to CEO John Lynch and his wonderful staff at the *San Diego Union-Tribune* and SignOn-SanDiego; Jim Fitzpatrick and the folks at *San Diego Magazine*, Ron Donohoo, San Diego Hall of Champions, Don Shelton at *The Seattle Times*, Kathy Davis and Chris Bartell at MLB.com, Mike Reilly in Battle Creek and Bob Kiesser in Long Beach.

Let's not forget John Skipper, George Bodenheimer and Kristen Hudak as well as Jerry Crasnick and Keith Olbermann at ESPN, Bill Plaschke at the *Los Angeles Times* and Jon Spoelstra in Portland.

How about Rick Redman at Hillerich & Bradsby, the wonderfully talented Bill Center of the San Diego Padres, Tyler Bergstrom of the Boras Corporation, Tom Bast of Triumph Books, Frank McGrath of the Indiana Pacers, John Gennaro, Bob Arboit in Seal Beach, Jack McCabe, the two and only Joe Jordan and Denny Dunne in San Diego, Fred Farrar and Tony Camara.

Our Anthology section would not exist except for the generosity of Dave Johnson (uncredited), Rich Herschlag and Peter Vegso at HCI Publications, Terry McDonnell at *Sports Illustrated*, Potomac Books and Josh Lewin, the fine people at Harcourt for Dick Williams and the baseball fanatics at McFarland in Jefferson, NC.

In addition, the publisher would like to thank the following for their contributions to this book: Bill Plaschke and Harcourt for the excerpt from *No More Mr. Nice Guy* by Dick Williams, P. J. Dragseth for *Eye for Talent* by McFarland, Rich Herschlag for *Before the Glory* with Billy Staples, Bill Center for *Padres Essential*. And to Lisa and Joe Liddy in Phoenix, Arizona for getting the words onto the pages and into book form.

CHAT ROOMS

PREFACE

It was a beautiful, sunny Monday morning in Cooperstown, New York, home of the National Baseball Hall of Fame. I was spending a dream summer there signing books until Labor Day, and I didn't have to pay anyone for the privilege.

Slowly at first, then like a rocket, word spread that Tony Gwynn had passed. The Tony Gwynn whose induction just a few years before helped generate—by far—the largest crowd in the history of the Hall of Fame. Fans wearing Padres paraphernalia were openly weeping and telling non-San Diego fans Tony Gwynn stories. Those stories from Padres faithful became the genesis of this book.

One of the biggest problems in doing a book about a person who has lived his or her life properly is constant repetition. Since this is a book of tributes from over 50 of Tony Gwynn's friends, obviously, there is going to be some repetition. Repetition is always a problem. For example, in my Mike Ditka book, seven people described a run Ditka made in Pittsburgh the week of JFK's assassination as the greatest run they had ever seen. Yet, only one of those made the book. The editor didn't understand that when the reader was through with the book, few would remember the importance or singularity of that catch and run; whereas, if most of the seven stories had remained intact, everyone would realize that one play summarized Ditka's persona and his career.

So, too, the repetition with Tony Gwynn, except many times greater. It was overwhelming. Almost eighty pages were deleted from this book because there were constant, similar or duplicate testimonials. Even so, many remained.

In doing almost four dozen books, I've never encountered as much repetition. It's a tribute to Gwynn, but a real challenge to the editors. On the other hand, there has never been a book that I worked on out of 49 books that was such a pleasure to hear stories about the subject.

Tony Gwynn was terrific.

When you find out more about Gwynn and how he achieved his success while keeping his values, you have to ask the question, "Why can't everybody live like Tony Gwynn?" There is nothing he did that was very difficult. He was very kind. He was hard working. He had all these values that everyone could possess if they desired.

It's unusual to talk about Tony Gwynn in the past tense because repeatedly, during interviews most of his friends, cohorts and colleagues would talk about him in the present tense.

I only write books on people who seem admirable from a distance. The fear, once you start a project, is the subject will turn out to be a jerk. As you will soon find out, you would want your son, your brother, your husband or your friends to possess these qualities of humbleness, thoughtfulness, joy for living, a passion for his job and the love of life that Tony Gwynn had.

Growing up on a farm in Iowa, I avidly read all the Horatio Alger-style books of John R. Tunis, the Frank Merriwell collection and Clair Bee's Chip Hilton series, all which preach the values of hard work, perseverance, obedience and sportsmanship where sooner or later, one way or another, some forlorn, underweight underdog would succeed beyond his wildest dreams in the arena of life. Frank Merriwell, thy name is Tony Gwynn. Tony Gwynn was better than Frank Merriwell. He was real life...more natural than Roy Hobbs...a Rudy with talent. Gwynn was manna from heaven to MLB and every other beleaguered professional sports league.

From the age of ten, I've been a serious collector of books, mainly sports books. During that time—for the sake of argument, let's call it thirty years—my favorite book style is the "eavesdropping" type where the subject talks in his own words... In his own words, without the 'then he said,' or 'the air was so thick you could cut it with a butter knife' waste of verbiage that makes it hard to get to the meat of the matter. Books like Lawrence Ritter's *The Glory of Their Times* or Donald Honig's *Baseball When the Grass was Real.* Thus I adopted that style when I started compiling the oral histories of the **VIN SCULLYS*** and Ron Santos of the world.

There is a big difference in doing a book on Mike Ditka or Harry Caray and doing one on Tony Gwynn. Ditka and Caray were much older than Gwynn, thus, they had many more years to create their stories and build on their legends. Furthermore, unlike Gwynn, they both liked to enjoy liquid fortification against the unknown, which leads to even more and wilder tales...and multiple divorces.

I don't even pretend to be an author. This book with its unusual format is designed solely for fans. I really don't care what the publishers, editors or critics think, but am vitally concerned that Gwynn fans have an enjoyable read and get their money's worth. Sometimes, the person being interviewed will drift off the subject, but if the feeling is that the reader would enjoy their digression, it stays in the book.

In an effort to include more material, the editor decided to merge some of the paragraphs and omit some of the punctuation which will allow for the reader to receive an additional 20,000 words—the equivalent of fifty pages. More bang for your buck... more fodder for English teachers...fewer dead trees.

It's also interesting—as you'll find in this book—how some people will view the same happening in completely different terms....There was a thought of omitting the attempts at humorous headlines—some of the headlines in this book

---

* For decades, the Chicago Cubs have had a guest sing "Take Me Out to the Ball Game" during the seventh inning stretch. Cubs organist Gary Pressly says that **VIN SCULLY** had the best singing voice of the over 3,000 warblers.

prove that truly great comedy is not funny—and eliminating some of the factoids since this book was written after Tony's death. But, all of Tony's friends who were questioned in this matter unanimously nixed that idea.

Tony Gwynn was a man in a society where orthodox behavior has stifled creativity, adventure and fun...a society where posturing and positioning one's image in order to maximize income has replaced honesty and bluntness... Tony Gwynn was a hero, a once-in-a-lifetime person...a principled man in a world of rapidly dwindling principles...a difference-maker on an indifferent planet...a man the way men used to be in an America that is not the way it used to be...a loyal man to colleagues, teammates and friends in an age when most people's loyalties are in the wallet...a man who fought the good fight and lived the good life.

We'll never forget Tony Gwynn because memories of people like Tony Gwynn never grow old.

Go now.

PROLOGUE

Billy Staple is a human Red Bull living in Nazareth, PA. Two decades ago he left a cushy job at AT&T corporate headquarters to teach in the projects of Bethlehem, PA. He has twice been nominated as Disney's National Teacher of the Year.

He would entice world famous athletes like Tony Gwynn, Derek Jeter, and Michael Jordan to come to his classroom and talk about life as they were growing up. Staples wondered if he could motivate hundreds of kids in one school in one town, why couldn't he do it with hundreds of thousands of kids nationwide? With that, a fabulous book, Before the Glory, *was born—a book that baseball fans loved—published by HCI—The Chicken Soup people.*

Throughout that effort he became friends with Tony Gwynn. Gwynn was enthusiastically supportive of Staples' efforts. Below Tony Gwynn relates to Billy Staples his adolescence in the Long Beach area.

My father, Charles Gwynn, was one of two boys and grew up in a modest house in Gallatin, Tennessee, which is about a half hour north of Nashville. He was considered an excellent athlete. His favorite sports were baseball and football. He was very analytical and intense, not only about his sports but about history, politics, you name it. As a young man, he spent most of the 1950s in the U.S. Army.

My mother, Vendella Douglas, was also born in Gallatin. Mom came from a larger family, with two sisters and four brothers. Her family owned a fairly big house with several acres of land which served as a small farm. My mom grew up with fresh eggs every morning straight out of the chicken coop. Mom was a good athlete too, especially in basketball and volleyball.

Mom and dad met and married in the mid–1950s and had their first child, Charles Jr., in 1958. My dad got out of the army around the same time. The following year, 1959, my father decided there were a lot more economic prospects for a young black family out west. So, not long after the Dodgers located there he took my mom and Charles Jr. to Los Angeles.

> We lived in a two-bedroom apartment, with Charles Jr. and me sharing a room.

I was born Anthony Keith Gwynn on May 9, 1960, in Los Angeles, California. We lived in a two-bedroom apartment, with Charles Jr. and me sharing a room. My dad worked in a warehouse for the State of California. Once I was big enough to walk and run around a little, Mom went to work for the post office in Los Angeles. Dad had the day shift. He would come home around six o'clock. My mother would have dinner ready, and then by around six-thirty she was out the door to work at the post office from 7 PM to 3 AM.

We had one car, a Chrysler 300. Dad drove it home, and Mom drove it right back out to work. It was like a tag team. During the week we were hardly ever all together at the same time. My favorite meal, as far as food goes, was dinner on Fridays, because we always had fish. My real favorite meals were any on Sunday or Saturday because we finally got to be together.

One Friday when I was about three–and–a–half, my mom was up and about in the early afternoon straightening the apartment and getting the fish ready in the kitchen. The TV was on in the living room and Mom ran in to watch because she heard there was a special report. Then she was crying, and I asked her why. She explained that the President of the United States—our president, John F. Kennedy—had been shot. The TV stayed on, and so did the special report. Mom went about cooking and everything, but she kept on crying.

Charles Jr. came home from school a little while later, and then Dad. Dad knew all about the President getting shot and that he had died in the hospital. Dad had all sorts of details about folks in Dallas who didn't like the President and how he shouldn't have been riding with the car roof down. My dad said this was bound to happen because Kennedy meant change, and some people would rather kill than see change. Dad was actually crying a little. I had never seen him cry over anything before.

Our little brother Chris was born on October 13, 1964. Mom stayed home a lot, which I really liked. But Dad said pretty soon Chris would be running around and we would need a bigger place. Not long after, we moved to another apartment in Los Angeles, this one was a duplex, with our apartment on the second floor and another family's on the ground floor. Charles Jr. and I were excited because there was a little yard with some grass in the back. While Mom was upstairs taking care of Chris, we'd go back there and invent games.

Most of our games involved a basketball and a trash can, which was our hoop. We'd put the trash can against the back wall of the building, and suddenly had a backboard. We played a lot of 21 and H-O-R-S-E. In H-O-R-S-E, we had to match each other's shot or get a letter. Once you had five letters, you lost. I learned how to shoot by watching Charles Jr., who we usually just called Junior. Junior was a right-hander. He would guide the ball with his left hand and use his right to get the ball up in the air. I watched him use that left-hand to put a little backspin on the ball. It worked. The ball would hit the back of the can and roll in instead of bouncing out wildly. As a left-hander, I did the same thing in reverse.

It was a pretty safe neighborhood. My big thrill was when dad sent me down the block to the store to get him some RC Cola. He gave me a dollar or two, and I brought back the change. One time I saw a piece of gum just beneath the counter. So I just put it in my pocket, paid for Dad's RC Cola, got the change, and walked home.

A few minutes after I gave Dad his soda and change, he saw me chewing the gum and asked me how I got it. When I looked at him, there was no way I could lie. I told him I took the gum. I had to spit it out into his hand. He told me stealing was wrong whether it was a million dollars or a tiny piece of candy.

I followed Dad downstairs and outside. There was a bush right out front, and he pulled a switch from it. Even before we went back upstairs, I knew that switch was headed for my behind. In the old apartment it was always the belt. I'd take the belt any day over the switch. I knew there was no chance of that bush out front ever dying. I wasn't sure so sure I liked this new apartment.

> My big thrill was when dad sent me down the block to the store to get him some RC Cola.

My favorite time of the year was summer, because that's when we would take our family vacation to Tennessee. My parents would take about 10 days off. We'd spend two days on the road driving there, six days there, and two days driving back to California. The way my parents' schedules were, that trip was the most time we would get to spend together, all five of us as a family.

Our Chrysler 300 had plenty of room for Junior, Chris, and me in the back. It was a powerful, solid car with an eight–cylinder engine, and it ate up the road. Sometimes I'd look over the top of the front seat at the speedometer, and it would read seventy or eighty miles an hour. But it didn't really feel like we were moving that fast.

We would take U.S. Route 66 and the highway that was gradually replacing it, Interstate 40, all the way from southern California to the middle of Tennessee. The open road was an amazing sight. In Arizona and New Mexico, we drove through desert for a hundred miles here, a hundred miles there. You could see perfectly clear for miles and miles, not like L.A. It was awesome how big America really was. I knew one day I'd get my own car, and I would love driving it about as far as I could go.

Dad was always talking to us about history and things like that back home, but on the road we could all talk about anything we wanted for as long as we wanted, with no interruptions. Mom and Dad both felt very strongly about Martin Luther King Jr. and the civil rights movement. They told us that where we were headed, Tennessee, was not like L.A.

Not that L.A. was perfect. It wasn't. But back where Mom and Dad came from, people were beaten up just for being black. People were lynched just for being black. To Mom and Dad, these weren't just stories. They were people they knew, people their families knew.

To Dad, baseball wasn't just baseball. Baseball was American history. Dad told us everything from Ty Cobb and Babe Ruth up through Ted Williams, Willie Mays, and the Giants and Dodgers both moving to California. But there was a special place in Dad's heart for Jackie Robinson of the Brooklyn Dodgers.

When Robinson was called up to the Dodgers in 1947, he would be facing some of the greatest pitching of all time in the thick of one of the greatest baseball rivalries of all time. But baseball was the easy part. Facing such intense racism and not being allowed to strike back or answer back for years would wear down any proud man. Jackie Robinson underwent incredible stress. That was something my father knew a lot about.

In Gallatin, we were lucky because we had both sets of grandparents. My father's father, Thomas Gwynn, was a quiet man. We loved my grandparents on my dad's side, but we wound up wanting to spend more time at the Douglas house, with Mom's parents. Over there we had acres to run around. Black walnuts fell to the ground, and we would use them to play catch and have batting practice.

It was like a paradise for us kids to be able to run about as far as we wanted in any direction. We took our own eggs from the chicken coops and made them for breakfast, just like Mom did when she was growing up. We ate ham from the hogs, and no doubt it tasted better than what we got at home. Mom said the world was changing, but not much had changed here.

Not my granddaddy George either. Granddaddy George was always great to us kids, taking us all over the farm and showing us things. He was kind of a big kid himself. At night he liked to drink a little, and he made no apologies for it. He wouldn't go out to drink. He was a family man. He'd sit there sipping his whiskey and talking up a storm. Eventually he'd start to repeat himself or make a little less sense than usual and know he'd had enough. So he would get up, head off to bed, and say, "Good night, kids."

Junior, Chris, and I shared one bedroom. Chris, the littlest, got the rollout bed. Junior and I had a bunk bed. Junior got the bottom bunk, and I got the top one. In the morning we would collapse the rollout bed and roll it under Junior's bunk.

The pecking order was a little different when it came to sports. Out back we would play Wiffle Ball. Dad would pitch to us whenever he had the chance, but Junior was the one teaching me mechanics from the beginning. Again, it was a righty–lefty thing. Dad was just happy to see us get out and play. Junior was the one I mirrored. He had Dad's intense personality and took it upon himself to show me how to wait on the ball and drive it.

Dad's intensity really seemed to come out in front of the TV. Every fall Sunday at our house we'd be sitting down with Dad to watch the **LOS ANGELES RAMS***. The Rams in those years —'67, '68, '69—had a great team but were not as dominant as the Green Bay Packers. Dad's favorite Ram, without question, was Deacon Jones. On the field Jones was a tough, mean defensive end who would punish the opposition. He not only invented the term quarterback "sack," he did it again and again. Jones was part of the "Fearsome Foursome"—Merlin Olsen, Rosie Grier, and Lamar Lundy—who as a unit struck terror in the hearts of the other team.

---

*The St. Louis Rams, once the **LOS ANGELES RAMS**, and prior to that the Cleveland Rams got the nickname from the Fordham Rams....The L.A. Rams were the first pro team to have a logo on their helmet.

Our house on Sundays was like a football clinic. Dad would yell at the screen, "Watch the blitz!" "Here comes the draw play!" "See that, Junior, you have to tackle low, not high. At the knees, with your shoulder." Junior wanted to play Pop Warner Football. I wasn't sure so sure I wanted to get hit like that.

Nineteen-sixty-eight was a hard year. Junior and I were restless to get out of the house and play organized sports. We'd see neighborhood kids walking around with shoulder pads and uniforms during football season. During baseball season, the same kids had Little League uniforms with stirrups. Sometimes instead of stirrups, it was socks with lines painted down the sides.

> Our house on Sundays was like a football clinic.

We wanted a part of that and felt like we needed to bust out of the backyard. We bugged Dad about it, and he agreed. He told us he'd work it out soon, and to hang in there. To tide us over, Dad dug his old baseball glove out of storage and gave it to us. It was a Ted Williams model. It was a righty glove, so Junior more or less inherited it. Not that I minded. It was in pretty bad shape anyway.

On Thursday, April 4, I was walking home from school and heard on the street Martin Luther King Jr. had been shot and killed. I knew Mom would be very upset, and when I walked upstairs and opened the door to our apartment, she was crying her eyes out. She gave me a big hug, and I could hear the TV on in the living room. Junior came home soon after. When Dad got home, he went through a lot of emotions. He wanted to make sure we were safe at home, because there were already riots going on in parts of Los Angeles. There was no sitting down in front of the TV that night, at least not for Dad. He stood and paced a lot.

Dad talked about how Dr. King had just the night before given his "I have been to the mountaintop" speech and sounded like he knew he was going to die. Dad thought the civil rights movement might die with Dr. King, because it wasn't clear America could really be civil. And as if Mom and Dad needed any more grief that evening, they were devastated that Dr. King had been killed in Memphis, right in their home state of Tennessee.

Two months later Robert F. Kennedy was killed, and it seemed my parents were living the nightmare all over again. This time it happened at the Ambassador Hotel in Los Angeles, only a few minutes from our apartment. Kennedy wasn't black, but my Dad said hardly anybody had fought harder for black people or for any American who suffered under prejudice. Dad said evil people took the lives of those who gave folks hope, because when you took away someone's hope, you took away his will to struggle. I saw hope drain from my parents, but certainly not all of it. They did believe in a Higher Power. They did have faith.

That summer we got a phone call and learned that Grandpa Thomas, Dad's father, had passed away suddenly back in Tennessee. He had had a heart attack. When we saw my parents crying, naturally we cried too—Junior, myself, and even little Chris. Mom and Dad were not angry at all. Dad did not lecture us. He just missed his dad and wished he was back home. He took it hard. As for my brothers and myself, we didn't really understand it. We never had had a death in the family before. To us, Grandpa Thomas still lived in Tennessee.

I had a Sting-Ray bike with a banana seat when I was nine. The deal was I got the bike to go to the store. I was Mom and Dad's store guy. But there was no way I was getting a basket with it, because that was for sissies. I'd rather carry groceries under my arm.

Of course, I got to ride the bike for fun, too. After school, I rode up and down the block a lot. One day I was riding along the sidewalk right in front of our apartment. Just as I passed our Chrysler 300 parked in the driveway, Chris came out of nowhere, and I slammed into him. The handlebars hit his face, and he flew backwards to the cement. He was bleeding a lot from his face, and I felt terrible. I dropped the bike, got down, and lifted him up. He was crying, and I had had enough crying for a long, long time.

I told Chris to calm down, it was going to be okay. I put my hand over his cheek, right where it was bleeding, to try to slow it down. I carried him upstairs like that and opened the door. I told Mom and Dad, "I hit Chris with the bike, but it was an accident." They yelled and said, "Why don't you look where you're going? You're going to get a whupping."

I stayed at home with Junior while they took Chris to the hospital. He came home with five stitches in his face. I didn't want my butt to end up looking like Chris's face. My parents, though, had had time to think about it, and they were calm when they walked in the door. On the way up to the apartment, they had talked to Chris and taken a good look at the layout of the driveway. They knew there was no way I could have seen Chris, and that was the end of it.

A few weeks later Mom and Dad told us they had thought it over for a long time and decided we were going to buy a house. They had picked one out in Long Beach, about twenty miles south of where we were. We would be near a park and even have a real backyard all on our own. That sounded incredible to me. But it was 1969, the year men walked on the moon, and anything was possible.

Our backyard at the house in **LONG BEACH*** was big enough for a baseball catch but not really big enough for baseball batting practice. So we invented a game called sockball. We would take a pair of tube socks, the ones with the fat stripes on them, and wrap them with a few rubber bands. That was a sockball. You could hit the heck out of a sockball, and it wouldn't go all that far, maybe seventy-five or a hundred feet.

*When the city of **LONG BEACH** wanted to name a field after him, Tony Gwynn said he would participate only if they named the field after the entire family.

Junior and I would pick broken wood bats out of the trash and nail them back together. Then we were ready for sockball. Our backyard was a lot longer than it was wide. So if you stood with your back to the house, left field was short. For me and Chris, the lefties in the family, it meant we had to be pull hitters if we didn't want to lose our sockball. A little over from left field, in what we called center, were a couple of trees. Over the trees was a home run, and we still had our sockball.

We also played figball. There were fig trees in the neighborhood, and the figs were about the size of a racquetball but sort of pear-shaped. The figs would fall to the ground in the spring, but you didn't want to use them in a game or batting practice right away. If they weren't ripe, they would burst when you hit them. All of this white gooey stuff would come out. So figball season started later in the spring, when the figs ripened and hardened.

In 1970 I turned ten, and Junior was eleven going on twelve. Junior decided he was going to join Little League, and Dad had it figured out. The games were on weekdays, so Junior would come home from school and get his uniform on right away. Dad would get home from work a little early and take Junior to the field. Chris and I had to stay home and take care of our home-work, and Mom would need the car back around supper. There wasn't much time to spare for Dad, but he was going to make it happen.

By five-thirty or six, Chris and I couldn't stand it anymore. We wanted to know how Junior's team did. Dad and Junior would walk in the door, and we'd yell, "Well, how'd you guys do?" And every time, Junior would shout, "We won!" We'd yell, "All right!" For us it was like the Dodgers won that night. Better. Junior pitched and played third base, sometimes first base. We would want to know every detail. If he pitched, what was work-ing for him, the fastball or curve? If he played third, did he snag any balls down the line like Brooks Robinson? And of course, we wanted to know how many hits he got and where they were.

We celebrated in our house sixteen straight times. Junior's team made it all the way to the Long Beach Little League championship. But when the door opened that night, we knew something was different. There was no noise from Dad and Junior in the driveway. They lost in the championship game. Chris and I were crushed, maybe more than even Junior was. But Dad, a true Dodger fan, said, "Wait till next year!"

> That was a sockball. You could hit the heck out of a sockball...

Junior set the standard for me and Chris. If he could compete, so could we. And Dad was one step ahead of us. At Friday night dinner, he and Mom were talking about finally getting a second car. Dad had always wanted a Cadillac. But this was strictly a practical decision, and one evening Dad came rolling home with a Datsun B210 four-door. There was one door for each of the four men, and Mom could still drive the Chrysler to work. The Datsun opened up a whole new world for us kids. It was even better than the new house.

Dad took us to nearby Silverado Park to watch semi-pro baseball games. We got to go to a couple of Rams exhibition games in the summer. But during the summer our mainstay was **DODGER STADIUM***. We would drive north up Interstate 110, past the Coliseum, to Chavez Ravine about once every couple of weeks. I insisted on going early so I could see infield and batting practice from the pavilion. Once Willie Davis trotted out there, my eyes were glued to him. He was a lefty like me. He was a Gold Glove centerfielder with a cannon of an arm. He could hit the

---

***DODGER STADIUM**—since the day it opened in 1962—is the only current stadium that has never changed its seating capacity. Because of a conditional use permit from the city of Los Angeles, the capacity is always 56,000....Fenway Park's seating capacity is lower for day games (36,984) than for night games (37,400).

home run here and there, but you rooted for him to steal bases, stretch a single into a double, and a double into a triple.

With the Datsun, Dad not only signed Junior up for Pop Warner Football in the fall, he became Junior's coach. Dad knew everything about the game, and Junior ate it up. Chris and I came along to the games and practices. One of the first things I noticed was the dummy drill. You have to stand there like a dummy with your arms open and get tackled at full speed. Junior didn't mind being on either side of that drill. I could take watching, but again, I didn't know if I wanted to get hit like that. I was no dummy.

By the time I was eleven, I was in Little League and the city youth baseball league too. I wasn't ready to commit to football, and Dad didn't push me. Instead, I would play in rough touch football games with my friends in the park. One Saturday afternoon I was running the ball up the middle, and one of the guys on defense was half laid out on the ground in front of me. As I hurdled over him, another defender clipped me and spun me. The ball was in my left arm, and I fell hard and off balance on my right arm. I had to push myself up with my left arm, because I couldn't bend my right arm. I knew something was wrong. I ran to my Sting-Ray and rode home, steering with my left arm. Mom took one look at my right arm and said it was broken.

At the hospital, the X-ray technician walked into the room and let everyone know my mom was correct. My arm was broken just below the elbow. The nurses had the arms stretched out on the table and started getting ready to wrap it. Nearby they were preparing bandages with plaster of Paris, so I knew I would be getting a cast. Then the doctor walked in, grabbed the X-rays, held them up to the light, and said, "Tell you what, Tony. Let's have a look at your arm over here."

He and the nurses moved me to another table with a heavy steel machine over it. Before I could ask what it was for, the doctor yanked down the machine on my elbow and I screamed. I nearly shot out of the seat, and that's when I realized the nurses were holding me down. "I'm sorry, Tony," the doctor said, "We had to rebreak it before we could set it." "Why didn't you tell me?" I yelled. "Why didn't you tell me?" But I knew why. If they had told me, I would have been long gone.

I did get a cast, and it stayed on for six weeks. It was an elbow cast, and I got used to doing almost everything with one hand. When the cast came off, it was a few more weeks before I could flex the elbow normally. I was anxious to get back into action. I had missed a lot of sockball and a lot of basketball. As far as football was concerned I was officially retired.

By the time I was in Stevens Junior High in Long Beach, our bedroom was exploding with the 1970s. The walls were plastered with covers and photos cut out of **SPORTS ILLUSTRATED***. In basketball, there were Lakers—Wilt Chamberlain, Jerry West, Gail Goodrich—and other superstars like Kareem and Dr. J. Our baseball wall lineup included **REGGIE JACKSON*** Vida Blue, Reggie Smith, and Dusty Baker. My brothers had dozens of football photos on the walls, especially now that Chris was a linebacker in Pop Warner. We would see something we liked, cut it out, get the masking tape, and bam, it was up on the wall. After a while, there was hardly enough room left for the window.

My parents controlled the TV most of the time, so we watched a lot of *Colombo, Mission Impossible*, and *Mannix*. Like a lot of TV shows, *Columbo* was set in L.A., but not in our neighborhood. When my brothers and I took over on Friday nights, we liked

---

* *SPORTS ILLUSTRATED* first published in 1954 and its first swimsuit issue was in 1964. The *Sports Illustrated Swimsuit Issue* has 52 million readers, 16 million of them are females...12 million more than normal...

---

*In **REGGIE JACKSON**'s last ten October games, he was 7 for 44 with one home run and 14 strikeouts...Only 3 of "Mr. October's" 18 October home runs put his team in the lead.

Sanford and Son, which was sent in the Watts section of Los Angeles, the poorer end of the spectrum. The show starred Redd Foxx and was about a feisty old junk dealer and his incredibly tolerant son. There was nothing on the planet funnier than Fred Sanford and his sister-in-law Aunt Esther going at it.

Probably my favorite possession that had nothing to do with sports was the cassette tape recorder my parents bought me. I used to tape songs right off the radio all the time. I didn't know exactly when the song was going to begin or end, so I always wound up missing a piece or recording a piece of something else. I figured out how loud to make the radio and how close to put the microphone to make the recording clear, sort of. And I told everyone around to be quiet, I was taping. It wasn't exactly high-tech, but it worked.

I wasn't the type of guy to sit down and listen to something for too long. I was always doing something while listening. My favorite thing was to play ball in the backyard while listening. If a Lakers game was on, I was listening to Chick Hearn. If a Rams game was on, it was Dick Enberg. But if there was no game on, I would crank up my taped songs while I played ball.

My dad was a big fan of smooth jazz—Grover Washington, George Benson, David Sanborn, Herb Alpert, Chuck Mangione. That was great music but a little mellow for me. I liked Parliament-Funkadelic, Stevie Wonder, Sly and the Family Stone. My parents put up a basketball hoop in the backyard for us. My paradise was cranking up the funk and shooting hoops back there. At Stevens, I was a point guard and thinking about the next level. Funk and the backyard hoop were going to get me there.

Long Beach Polytechnic High School was about as racially balanced as possible—around 25 percent black, 25 percent white, 25 percent Latino, and 25 percent Asian, most of whom were of Japanese origin. We were also sort of balanced in the types of students we had, and I was kind of a nerd. I had friends and acquaintances who on a Friday night were looking to find a party and get drunk or high. I avoided all that. First of all, I didn't want to disappoint my parents, especially after everything they had done for us. And second, I felt I was going to have some great chances, and those chances could be ruined by bad decisions.

That didn't mean I didn't want to date. But I was shy. It could take me all day or all week to muster up the courage to talk to a girl. The one girl I could talk to easily, Alicia, lived down the street from us. She was on the short side with black hair, brown eyes, and glasses, but she was cute with those glasses. She also happened to be very athletic, and that gave us a lot to talk about.

I had played Little League against her younger brother, and we used to pummel them all the time. So I would rag on her and she she would rag on me. "We're going to kick your brother's butt Saturday." "Not unless y'all cheat some more." She talked a lot of yin, and I talked a lot of yang. I felt comfortable with Alicia, but I was still shy. She was very outgoing, had lots of friends, and was a year older than me. She was out of my league.

During the school year, my parents let me focus on sports. They knew how important sports were to me. But over the summer, I worked. One year I put my name into a pool at Silverado Park. I got lucky. My name was pulled to coach softball. My responsibilities included running the field, painting foul lines, and picking up litter from the field. I could think of worse jobs. Another summer I was on the Poly paint crew. We went to public schools in Long Beach and painted bleachers, lines on tennis courts, and that sort of thing.

> In high school, sports was my way to break down barriers.

In high school, sports was my way to break down barriers. It was not so much about painting lines as about crossing them. But if I was going to go to college, I knew I needed to do a better job in class. First semester junior year, I did, and I had a little help. Mr. Tankenson was a history teacher with the most popular elective at Poly. Everyone wanted to get into his American history class, but there was a long waiting list. By the luck of the draw, I got in. Some kids tried to crash the class, but the administration wasn't having it.

Mr. Tankenson was a short white guy, Jewish, with sort of an Afro. He was cool. He was one of us. He was funny and spoke to us like adults. Usually a history class was chockful of names and dates from hundreds of years ago. But on the first day of class, Mr. Tankenson give us an outline. We would be starting with 1960, the year I was born, and then moving forward.

When Mr. Tankenson talked about why John F. Kennedy was so loved at the same time he was so hated, I could relate to it. I remembered my mom's reaction to the assassination. When Mr. Tankenson talked about the relationship between the **VIETNAM WAR*** and the Cold War, I could remember my dad sitting in front of the TV talking about the same thing. I hadn't always been paying all that much attention to what Dad was saying, but somehow the words were still implanted in my brain, and now I was starting to make the connection. History became a lot more alive for me in that class. As a result I was not only doing well in history, but better in my other classes, too.

Mr. Tankenson gave assignments that were out of the ordinary. One day he said, "Your homework for tomorrow is to bring in a record that describes who you are and what you think. Tell us about the song and why that song is you." I knew the record I wanted to bring in, an album called *Ubiquity* by the vibe artist Roy Ayers. Dad's taste in jazz had started to seep in. The song I was going to play was "Life Is Just a Moment." That was the way I felt. Life was a series of moments, and if you didn't take care of business, it was going to be gone.

*Nolan Ryan is the last major leaguer to lose playing time due to **MILITARY SERVICE**.

The next day in class, I waited my turn and scribbled some final notes. Mr. Tankenson had brought in a portable stereo so each student could play their record and then talk about it. I was batting around seventh. I had *Ubiquity* in my hand and was ready to go. Then as one of the guys in the class walked up to the stereo, I saw the album he was carrying—*Ubiquity* which, strangely, means everywhere. There were a bunch of other songs on the album, but as he put down the needle, I heard the first few notes of "Life Is Just a Moment." For me, a big moment had come and gone.

Alicia had a Volkswagen with big tires and a stick shift. When I got my learner's permit, she let me drive the VW under her watchful eye. The first time I drove it, I went up on the curb, and Alicia helped me get back down. My basketball coach, Coach Palmer, was also my driver's ed instructor. Coach Palmer had to tell me more than once to keep my hands on the wheel. In Los Angeles or thereabouts, that was good advice. The last day of class, there were four students in the car. We had to take turns driving on the freeway. I kept my hands on the wheel, managed not to jump any curbs, but decided to log some more miles before taking my road test.

Charles Jr. was now in **COMPTON COLLEGE*** and considering a baseball scholarship at California State University, Los Angeles. He had dropped football in high school to focus on baseball and thought I should do the same. He turned me on to *The Science of Hitting* by Ted Williams, and I became a more selective, thoughtful hitter as a result. Junior also could be found in our backyard most days lifting weights with a set he had bought using money from a summer job. I was kind of skinny, but weights weren't my thing. Baseball wasn't my main thing either.

*Hall of Famer Duke Snider and NFL Commissioner Pete Rozelle were high school basketball teammates in **COMPTON**.

Basketball was definitely my thing. The guys on our team were role models for me as much as my brother was. We had three All-Americans on that team. Johnny Nash was a six-feet-seven small forward headed to Arizona State University. Michael Wiley was a six-feet-nine center headed to Long Beach State University. And James Hughes was a six-feet-five forward recruited by the University of Washington. These guys were getting letters from colleges every day. They stayed away from any kind of trouble, especially as seniors. All they wanted to do was win a championship and go to college. And all they needed was something stupid like getting busted for smoking pot to ruin that.

> All of a sudden, my nerdiness changed to hipdom.

I wanted a championship too. And I wanted to go out with Alicia. It seemed like time was running out on both. Alicia was headed to UCLA in the fall. I felt like courage wasn't going to get it done for me. So I came up with an idea. One day I was talking to Alicia and made a bet with her. Dorsey was number one in Los Angeles, and we were number one in the CIF. Before we played Dorsey, I told Alicia, "If we beat 'em, you've gotta go out on a date with me. If we lose, you can keep pummeling me like you've been pummeling me all these years." She said, "Okay, cool."

With the help of our three All-Americans, Poly won, and Alicia had to pay up. Dad give me $10 for the date, which was a record for him. I took Alicia to **DENNY'S*** for dinner, and we had a great time. Back at school, things seem to change the next day because of one date. All sorts of people who had cheered for me on the court but never stopped to say hello were now stopping to say hello and more. All of a sudden, my nerdiness changed to hipdom. Alicia had taken me to a new level.

---

*An Atlanta **DENNY'S** inaugurated the Grand Slam Breakfast in 1977...and named it to honor Henry Aaron.

Chapter One

LET'S GO AZTECS

Meet the Aztecs

RICK BARLOW
Outfield
6-1, 175, R-R, Junior

Has worked his way up from a walk-on JV player to a potential starting centerfield position this year...Could be the team's fastest player...Played 31 games, all in the infield, last year and is now making transition to center...Hit .182...Stole six bases in seven tries...Had one homer and a pair of two-hit games...All-State high school basketball player...High school: Groveton (NH)...Summer ball: San Diego Thoroughbreds (.342)...Hometown: Groveton, NH...Undeclared major...Born: 10/12/60.

JIM GOERTZ
Utility Infielder
5-10, 160, L-R, Sophomore

A major contribution to this year's varsity by last year's junior varsity...Second on JV's in hitting last year (.333), first in doubles (11), and third in RBI's (18)...Can steal a base and has a good eye at the plate...Was JV's Most Valuable Player...All-League and All-County in high school...High school: Grossmont...Summer ball: Barrhead, Canada (.315)...Hometown: San Diego...Accounting major...Born 10/16/61.

CURTIS BURKHEAD
Pitcher
6-2, 200, R-R, Senior

Injured most of last year and pitched only 40 innings...Was team's number one pitcher in 1979 with record-setting 10-0 mark...Did not have the control which made him great in 1979...Was All-WAC and All-Rocky Mountain in 1979...Could be a key to this team...Is pencilled back in the starting rotation this year...First collegiate win was a 1978 shutout of Wyoming...High school: Crawford (San Diego)...Drafted: Minnesota, 23rd round, 1977...Summer ball: Clarinda (IA)...Hometown: San Diego...Recreation major...Born 4/9/59.

Year	G-GS-CG	IP	H	R	ER	BB	SO	W	L	SV	ERA
1978	18- 8- 4	66	62	30	18	42	42	4	7	1	2.45
1979	16-13- 4	76⅔	62	30	20	28	49	10	0	0	2.35
1980	13- 7- 1	39⅔	39	26	16	27	22	2	2	0	3.63
Totals	47-28- 9	182½	163	86	54	97	113	16	9	1	2.67

TONY GWYNN
Outfield
5-11, 180, L-L, Junior

Possibly the team's best pure natural hitter...Will not play baseball until March when basketball ends...Starting point guard for basketball team, having led the WAC in assists the past two years...Remarkable year in 1980: .423 with one extra base hit per 6.5 at bats...Very fast and hits to all fields with surprising power...Had two or more hits in 17 of his 41 games...Had a ten-game hitting streak in which he swatted .517 and carries a six-game spree into 1981...Will play centerfield and DH...High school: Long Beach Poly...Summer ball: Boulder, CO (.400)...Hometown: Long Beach, CA...Recreation major...Born 5/9/60.

Year	G	AB	R	H	DB	TR	HR	RBI	BB	SO	SB-A	AVG.
1979	34	73	17	22	4	1	1	11	8	5	4- 8	.301
1980	41	130	30	55	10	4	6	29	12	7	13-14	.423
Totals	75	203	47	77	14	5	7	40	20	12	17-22	.379

JOE FERRANTE
Pitcher
6-5, 210, R-R, Senior

Among top four starters last year, but needs consistency to hold down that position...Was not hit hard, but walked nearly one per inning...Has excellent potential...Did not suffer a loss after the team's eighth game of the year...High school: Camden...Junior college: San Jose CC...Hometown: Campbell, CA...Psychology major...Born 10/5/59.

Year	G-GS-CG	IP	H	R	ER	BB	SO	W	L	SV	ERA
1980	11-10- 0	41⅓	34	35	24	38	29	2	2	0	5.36

NICK HARSH
Pitcher
6-2, 190, R-R, Junior

Hopefully the year he'll fulfill his considerable promise...Has had injury problems for two years...Had some excellent games last season as member of regular starting rotation, but needed consistency...Won all four of his games in the last month of the season and continued that positive trend by going 8-1 in summer ball...Tossed 10-0 shutout over UCSD...High school: Mater Dei...Drafted: San Diego Padres, round six, 1977...Hometown: Santa Ana, CA...Criminal justice major...Born 8/8/59.

Year	G-GS-CG	IP	H	R	ER	BB	SO	W	L	SV	ERA
1978	9- 2- 0	23⅓	32	26	22	14	10	1	1	0	8.49
1979*	1- 1- 0	2	0	0	0	1	2	0	0	0	0.00
1980	12-10- 1	45	46	29	23	29	25	4	2	0	4.60
Totals	22-13- 1	70⅓	78	55	45	44	37	5	3	0	5.76
*redshirted											

MATT GIAMPAOLI
Pitcher
6-2, 200, L-L, Junior

Team captain at Skyline JC last year...Was 5-2 with 8 saves in his two seasons there...Projected as a reliever by the Aztecs...All-League in high school...Second team All-League football star in high school...High school: Burlingame...Summer ball: Abney A's, San Mateo (4-3, 3.13 ERA, 90 strikeouts in 87 innings)...Hometown: Burlingame, CA...Health science major...Born 12/16/59.

TIM LAMBERT
Pitcher
6-0, 165, R-R, Junior

Newcomer favored to win a job in the starting rotation...Comes from Citrus Junior College, where he was the team's Pitcher-of-the-Year with a 12-2 record and 2.20 ERA...All-League in J.C...As senior in high school, had 1.86 ERA and a .428 batting average...High school: Pomona...Drafted: Philadelphia, second round, 1980; Chicago Cubs, fifth round, 1980...Summer ball: Boulder, CO (3-0)...Hometown: Pomona, CA...Art major...Born 8/1/59.

8

TONY GWYNN WAS JUST A REGULAR GUY WHO SOME DAYS WORE A CAPE

NICK HARSH

Nick Harsh, a native of Santa Ana, was a standout athlete at Mater Dei High School before attending San Diego State University on a baseball scholarship. Out of high school, he was drafted in the sixth round by the Padres. After his senior year at SDSU he was drafted in the sixth round by the Kansas City Royals. He now lives in Malvern, Pennsylvania, just outside of Philadelphia, where he is a key employee at AstraZeneca.

At **MATER DEI***, I was a year ahead of Bobby Meacham. Bobby was later a teammate at San Diego State and a first-round pick of the St. Louis Cardinals. When I was a sophomore, we had a new coach, a guy named Bob Ickes. Bob was a young guy who started a summer team with just the high school guys. To keep all the guys together, we had to join a league in Long Beach. The name of the team was A. S. Cake Supply. One of the moms on the team owned a cake supply company so she sponsored the team. The league was based out of Blair Field in Long Beach. Many teams played at Blair Field—Mater Dei, Fleetwood High School, Long Beach Poly— it was the Joe DiMaggio Summer League.

> ***MATER DEI** is a sports powerhouse in Southern California. The Santa Ana school boasts former football players like USC quarterback Matt Barkley and Heisman winners John Huarte and Matt Leinart. Basketball alumni include Darryl Strawberry Jr., Miles Simon, Reggie Geary, and LeRon Ellis.

That's where we first met Tony. There were two very strong teams, our team, and Tony's team which was the Long Beach Jets. Their coach was John Rambo. John was an incredible man who was a high jumper in the 1964 **OLYMPICS**.* The way the league worked was whoever won the league went on to the next state level and the winner was allowed to pick three kids from any of the other teams.

During the post-season we played them, and these battles were unreal. The first year, Tony Gwynn's Jets won it and they picked up myself, Bobby Meacham, and a pitcher named Tom Croal.

Playing the Jets was just unbelievable. Tony was phenomenal. We were afraid. We were driving in there a couple of times a week, playing in their backyard. What we learned was they were the nicest guys in the world. They were just terrific and we got real close. There were great games. Their coach John Rambo was this huge big 6-foot 8-inch man with wonderful demeanor who was so committed to the kids.

When the Jets picked the three of us to go up to San Rafael to play in the state tournament, John Rambo's truck got broken into and we lost all the uniforms. John showed up and went, "We got nothing! I don't have any of the uniforms." We drove to an Oshman's Sporting Goods. We bought shorts, baseball sleeves, and just jerseys off the rack, some yellow hats, yellow socks, and yellow gloves.

Then we drove up to San Rafael, north of San Francisco, to play in this tournament. It was me and Tom in my brother's old Chevy van with Tony and a left-handed pitcher named Lonnie. Those other teams looked at us. This all-black team from Long Beach with a couple white guys. Tony was fantastic. I don't think he made an out. We lost in the championship game but it was just an amazing amount of fun.

*Baseball was a demonstration sport in the 1964 Tokyo **OLYMPICS**. Two decades later, it became an official Olympic sport.

When we went up to San Rafael for that **JOE DIMAGGIO*** tournament the racial overtones were really intense. There was a heavy, "Look at these black guys." I was one of just three white guys on the team, and I remember feeling so uncomfortable. I grew up in a very heavy minority situation.

When we drove home, coming down Interstate 5, Tony and Lonnie were in the back of the van. It was a Chevy van with carpet and two big bucket seats in the front. They were real popular in the mid-'70s. Two girls from Canada pulled up alongside of us and they're honking and waving. Tom and I are a couple of blond kids with long hair. Tom said "I think they want us to pull over." Tony was so funny. He said, "We can't pull over. If you pull over and we get out, they're gonna think we're gonna kill them." We pulled over and talked to them. They were going down to Disneyland and Knott's Berry Farm. They followed us as we dropped Tony and Lonnie off in the middle of Long Beach. My friend and I spent the week with them in Disneyland....

Tony was very shy. Back in high school and when we went to college together he was deathly shy. If it wasn't for Alicia, I don't think he'd ever have left the house or apartment. Alicia was very dynamic, very worldly, much more aware of the world and where they fit in, whereas Tony was innocent. When Tony left Long Beach as a youngster to go to tournaments or we went on the road in college, Tony would never leave hotels. We would have to bring him back food.

Baseball seemed easy for Tony from the time he was 14. His hand-eye coordination was phenomenal. I pitched pretty hard in high school, and nobody could hit my fastball. Tony would pull my fastball down the right field line. That just never happened when I was 16, 17, 18 with good stuff.

---

*To accentuate a wiggle in her walk, Marilyn Monroe would cut a quarter of an inch off one of her heels.... The combination on Monroe's jewelry box was 5-5-5— **DIMAGGIO's** uniform number.

Never once did I see Tony show any emotion. He was the best young player I ever saw. There was just nobody near him.

One time against us in high school, Tony was up. Tom Croal was pitching. Nobody could get a hit off Croal. I mean nobody! Tony hits the ball at me. It bounced about 10 feet in front of me on the outfield grass, and hits me straight in the forehead. I'm out. I'm on my back. I'm looking up. Tony's standing there, "Hey Nick. You all right?" I went, "What was that?"

He was unbelievable. It just doesn't happen, it just doesn't happen.

> "Absolutely not. You're not playing both sports. It's a one-sport scholarship."

Tony and I went down to San Diego State together. Tony went on a basketball scholarship and I went on a baseball scholarship. My freshman year I'd run into Tony. I told him, "These baseball guys are good but Tony I'm telling you, you should talk to someone about playing baseball." He actually went to the basketball coach, a guy named Tim Vezie. Vezie said, "Absolutely not. You're not playing both sports. It's a one-sport scholarship." I had told Coach Dietz about Tony—"This is a guy we need." That winter, we all went home for Christmas. Coach Dietz called me and said, "I talked to Coach Vezie. There's no way Tony can play baseball. Are you serious, he's that good of a player?" I said, "I can only tell you I've never seen a hitter like that."

We come back for the next year and Coach Vezie had left. They hired a new guy named Smokey Gaines, a black coach out of the University of Detroit. He was flamboyant, a really good guy. He knew what he had with Tony.

When the basketball season started, that would have been Bobby Meacham's freshman year '78-'79, Bobby went to Dietz and said, "This is just ridiculous. I'm telling you, Tony is the best player in the country." I had already been through it with Dietz, and Tony had already been told "no."

But then, Tony went to Smokey and said, "I really want to do this. After the season I want to go out for the baseball team, and see how it goes." The rest is history. He had a week of batting practice and in the first game he was 4 for 4 against USC. He was incredible and he never stopped hitting.

Every baseball team at San Diego State was special. Our last year, we were number one in the country most of the year. We ended up the regular season with 60 wins and 15 losses. Nine guys drafted, it was unbelievable. We got to the regional. We should've just absolutely wiped it out, but we lost two really close games. The last one was against Oral Roberts. They had pitcher Mike Moore who went straight to the majors.

The only emotion I ever saw from Tony was his last college at-bat. I was pitching, and thought, "Oh my God, Tony's up. This is going to happen." He hit the ball square on the nose, but the wind was blowing 30 miles an hour straight in against the ball in **OKLAHOMA***. The season was over and he was an angry guy. That ball went into the teeth of that wind and it went nowhere.

When we got beat in our last college game—they kicked us out of our hotel and we flew home. Out of nowhere, Tony told us he was going to get married. I said, "The least we can do is throw you a bachelor party." We had a party, and we played checkers with shot glasses full of water. That was Tony's bachelor party. It was so funny—pouring water and Sprite into shot glasses on the checkers table.

Alicia was fabulous. She was very smart, very articulate. She was very practical. Tony spent all his time at the basketball court, and Alicia ran track at San Diego State. There's a soft side to Alicia, but if you didn't know her, you wouldn't know

---

*When Troy Aikman was a senior at Henryetta (OK) High School, he was the **OKLAHOMA** Boys High School state typing champion.

it existed. Back then, I knew her pretty well and she knew me. We had a comfort zone. Our coach decided that part of our pitching conditioning would be that we'd run on the track. Start running 440s, 200s, miles for time. We didn't know that the track was reserved at that time for the SDSU women's track team. The first day we ran, Alicia came over and let us know exactly how it was going to work. I walked up to her and said, "Alicia, this is our bad." She says, "Alright, you take care of this, Nick. Just stay out of our way. Not a problem." I'll never forget that one. Nobody knew who she was. By the time I got over there, it was too late to tell everybody, "Hey this is Tony's girlfriend." She had her point made real quick, and we were back up on that track later.

> Alicia was fabulous. She was very smart, very articulate.

He and Alicia got married in a small Baptist church in Long Beach right near Blair Field. Blair Field is local landmark. It's often used as a location to film commercials. When the Rams moved to Anaheim the Rams practice facility was Blair Field. Blair Field is a park. It's one of those parks probably built in the '40s with an outdoor stage, barbecue pits, and a baseball field. It's a stadium-like field. When Tony got married, the church wasn't far from there. There were no plans for a reception because it was a really last-minute wedding. We didn't expect to get beat in Oklahoma. Tony knew he was going to get drafted, and he was going to go away. Alicia and Tony had been dating since they were about 14. She lived down the same street. So it was a last-minute thing.

We went to the wedding, and it was packed...afterwards we went to Ralph's Supermarket and got Cokes, some deli meat, bread, mustard, potato chips. We bagged it up and came back to the Blair Field Park. We went up on the stage and just hung out for a little bit, and had some sandwiches. Don't ever say that we didn't know how to throw a bachelor party or a heckuva wedding reception!...

Bobby Meacham was so good. Bobby had an over-the-top release and a cannon for an arm. Everybody on the field would watch Bobby and say, "Oh my God, that's a really great player." And he had so much power. Everything he did was rote. He ran like the wind. The problem with Tony was that he had played basketball and he had no exposure in the fall. That's really why he was drafted so much lower than Bobby Meacham. He didn't pick up a baseball bat until basketball finished in late February or early March. But Tony was flat out gifted. He was one of the better basketball players to come out of Long Beach Poly, and Long Beach Poly was a football and basketball factory. The baseball season at Poly wasn't their big deal. It was football and basketball. Tony was ungodly on the basketball court. He was unbelievable.

> The Royals had sent a telegram to my house, but it was delivered next door. The people next door didn't speak or read any English.

The draft was different back then. I was at home just waiting for a phone call. On draft day, we all just started calling each other to see if we were drafted. I lived in a predominantly Hispanic neighborhood. The Royals had sent a telegram to my house, but it was delivered next door. The people next door didn't speak or read any English. So it was a week after the draft before I heard anything. During that time I was really disappointed. It was really painful. My poor mom and dad, my brothers and sisters, they didn't know what to say to me. We had gone through the whole draft out of high school hoopla, scouts around negotiating and all that. All of a sudden, I thought I had to go out and get a real job.

Everyone else but me knew where they were going. Finally Coach Dietz called and said, "What do you hear?" I went, "I haven't heard anything, Coach." He goes, "Well I talked to one of the Houston scouts and he said he heard your name, and someone took you." I told him that I hadn't heard anything.

Finally, the Royals scout called and told me I had been drafted by the Royals.

I was a sixth round pick by the Royals. I went to Fort Myers for training, spent time in AA in Jacksonville, got traded to the **ASTROS***. I spent four and a half years in the minor league world. There was just nothing better. You move up a level and you get better, you move up another level and you get better. It's just an amazing feeling. I'd think, "Is this as good as I'm going to get?" It would get a little easier. Then, all of a sudden, it's not easier anymore and it ends.

Tony and I never crossed paths in the minors but certainly I knew he was tearing it up. Our hometown papers would make a weekly list of area minor leaguers and how they were doing. My dad would keep me in touch with how everybody was doing. Bobby Meacham was with the Cardinals and they were in the Florida State League so we saw a lot of each other. When Bobby went to AA, he ran into Tony.

When Tony went to the big leagues a year out of San Diego State it was an affirmation at every level. We figured out that we were pretty good. This was Tony's normal. It wasn't any surprise that Tony would adjust. He never ever had to adjust. There was no adjustment. I know whenever I moved up to the next level—when I went to AA—that was an adjustment. If you didn't make the adjustment fast, you were done. When you go to spring training and these big-league hitters are there, you're like, "Oh man, I can't miss by two inches anymore. I got to miss by a quarter of an inch to get away with it." Tony never had to adjust, so it wasn't a surprise that he moved up to the major leagues.

*Larry Dierker threw a no-hitter for the **ASTROS** in 1976 and was given a thousand-dollar bonus check by the team. He gave the money back because the team was in receivership saying "A no-hitter is a good enough reward for me."

Tony and I used to go back to San Diego State for the alumni game a lot. One year we rented a limo, put him in a limo, and drove him onto the field. That was pretty funny. After I got out of baseball, I moved to Northern California. After the Giants games, I'd wait for him, and we'd hang out together afterwards. In later years, he was coming to Williamsport with Harold Reynolds to broadcast Little League for ESPN. I got to spend a lot of time with him there sitting up in the stands and in between games. My boys got a chance to get to know him, go eat with him, and Tony was incredible. We did that three straight years. My boys were just in such awe of him. He was such a nice guy.

Tony remained grounded throughout his career. Alicia was so important for him early on in his life. She didn't allow him to stray. I just know Alicia wouldn't allow any bad influence on Tony. She was the best. Charles, his brother, was a very dedicated and directed individual. His mom and dad were so kind and they were just nice people.

God gives you certain gifts but it's what you do with those gifts that makes the difference. Tony was the best at that I ever saw even when he was 15 years old. Tony took it to the highest level possible. I think if Tony never looked at one video, read one book, or talked to **TED WILLIAMS*** one time, he'd still have been the greatest hitter ever. He respected the game and put in the work to make it happen.

*Gwynn was selected for the All-Star Game in 1999, but couldn't play because of injury. He went to Boston anyway, so he could take a few fly balls off the Green Monster and then be at the side of <u>TED WILLIAMS</u>, and steady him, as Williams threw out the game's first pitch.

WHEN WE WERE YOUNG
AND OUR WORLD WAS NEW

BOBBY MEACHAM

Bobby Meacham was drafted in the first round of the 1981 amateur draft by the St. Louis Cardinals out of San Diego State, two rounds ahead of teammate Tony Gwynn. In less than two years, he was in the major leagues with the New York Yankees. He spent six years with the Yankees and is now the manager of the New Hampshire Fisher Cats, in the Eastern League.

Tony was at San Diego State for a year already before I got there. I had played summer ball against Tony when we were in high school together. I was talking with head coach Jim Dietz one day and Tony walked by. Coach Dietz said, "Hey, Tony how are you?" I said, "Is that Tony Gwynn? I didn't know Tony played here." And coach told me he's not on the baseball team, he's on the basketball team. That's the first I knew of what happened to Tony after we played summer league in high school.

In that summer league, Tony played center field for that Long Beach team and he and his brother Chris were the best two players on the team. They used to wear purple and gold like the **LAKERS***. They even wore shorts. They wore shorts and knee-pads. It was funny watching guys wearing purple and gold with shorts on. I remember him being really skinny. To the point

*In March 1954, the **LAKERS** and the Hawks played a regulation, regular season NBA game using baskets that were 12' high rather than the usual 10'...the next night they played each other in a doubleheader. True facts, believe it or not!

where my cousin used to come and watch us play once in a while. I'd say to him, "Come and watch us play this weekend." He'd go, "Are you guys playing Mickey's team." To him, Tony Gwynn was Mickey Rivers, that type of player. A good swinger, a skinny guy, a good hitter. Tony would go fast and played like Mickey Rivers.

How good was Tony Gwynn back then? When I was talking with coach Dietz and I found out the Tony was not playing baseball, I said, "Coach, he's the best player I've ever played against." Coach said to me, "Well, there's a whole different level of baseball here." I was just stunned. Because, when you played the state tournament, you take the best players around you from the other teams and get a couple of them, and Tony was number one on the list. He was definitely at that age, in high school, the best player I've ever played against.

My friend, Nick Harsh, started our campaign to get Tony on the baseball team a year earlier. By the time I got there the following year we started right away telling coach, "Hey Coach, you got to get Tony to play baseball." That was when there were signs that the basketball coach was probably going to be leaving. That's when Tony started hitting in the cage after basketball games when they weren't practicing. It was probably a week before the season was over that he did that, and by then the coach was, "Well, why not?" All I remember is him stepping into a spot on the team right after basketball season was over. He didn't play all the time. He played probably two-thirds of the time, like a platoon mode. A couple of the players that he was actually platooning with were Kerwin Danley, who is now an MLB umpire, and Steve Sayles, who used to be a trainer for the Oakland A's.

Tony was hot right away. We always would joke about it. I would be frustrated. It was a couple of weeks into the season. Tony had played only a few games, whereas I had played 20 games and he already had more RBIs than me. He was automatic when he stepped on the field after basketball.

The first time I realized that he was having success after he was drafted by the Padres was during my second year in Instruction League right after the regular minor league season. It was in September. I was in a sports bar in St. Pete with a couple of teammates and a couple of coaches. We were watching the Braves playing the Padres. I saw Tony Gwynn on the TV and I said to my buddy, "That's my teammate from San Diego State, Tony Gwynn."

> When you went to pro ball... Why did you turn into a switch hitter?"

My hitting coach, Johnny Lewis, overheard me and asked, "Did you say you played with this kid in college?" I said, "Yeah, Tony Gwynn." He said, "Were you guys in the same draft?" I said, "Yeah." He looks at another coach, George Kissel, and said, "Hey George, we signed the wrong guy." They were joking with me all the time, "What the heck? How did we pass this guy up?" Tony was never not really good as a hitter. The reason he went as low as he did was because he didn't run well, he didn't throw well at all, and he wasn't in baseball shape. But besides that, he was a polished hitter all the time and he just got better and better.

It was just amazing when I saw him at the plate against the Braves. I was just beaming that one of our San Diego State guys had made it. His dream had come true and he had made it to the big leagues. When my friends and I were in high school, that's all we talked about, making it to the big leagues.

It never shocked me how good Tony became. I believed in myself. I thought I was going to be really really good. I thought I had a chance to be as good as any shortstop in baseball, and I thought he was a better player than I was.

We were pretty good on road trips. We didn't get into trouble. The only thing I remember about Tony was his bad eating habits. He'd fill up on Coca-Cola, chips, and candy. That was his food on road trips.

For me the thing I remember most about Tony is him laughing. He was just smiling and laughing all the time.

The final thing I remember is when I came out to San Diego for the Hall of Fame thing. He knew I had to fly back home so Tony said, "Let me take you to the airport." On the way, he said to me, "Do you mind me asking you a question?" I said, "What's that, Tony?" He said, "We played together for three years at San Diego. When you went to pro ball, why did you switch hit? Why did you turn into a **SWITCH-HITTER***?" I said, "Oh man, that's a long story. That's one of the worst decisions I ever made." He said, "You could handle it." I said, "Yeah man, I don't know. I tried to do something new and different. I thought it would be good for my career."

All those years ago when we were playing at San Diego State, if someone had told me that I'd be a first-round pick of the St Louis Cardinals and play many years at Yankee Stadium, I'd have said, "You're probably right." If they told Tony that he'd go down as one of the greatest hitters ever and be in the Baseball Hall of Fame, he'd probably laugh and say, "Yeah, right!"

That was our personalities. I had a belief in myself and Tony was always laughing. Smiling and laughing and having a good time.

He's probably got Heaven smilin' now!

---

*In 1995, in the space of four days, Ken Caminiti became the first **SWITCH HITTER** in major league history to homer from both sides of the plate, in the same game, three times in a season.

HOOPS THERE IT IS:
GYM DANDY

TIM VEZIE

Tim Vezie was the person responsible for bringing Tony Gwynn to San Diego. As head basketball coach at San Diego State he recruited Gwynn out of Long Beach Poly High School to be his starting point guard for the Aztecs. Vezie now lives in Bend, Oregon. His father, Manny Vezie, played under Knute Rockne at Notre Dame and coached with Rockne prior to Rockne's death. His mother is 108 years old and is still alive and vital in Redding, California.

I wanted Tony Gwynn because he was one heck of an athlete. He was a great basketball player. I've always believed that basketball was his first primary love of a game. He was a real leader on the floor in high school and he led his team as a junior to the championship round. At the time I wasn't really aware of his baseball ability. I didn't really explore that possibility, because I wanted him to come to play basketball at San Diego State and be our future point guard.

I denied Tony the ability to play baseball. I said, "No. You can't play baseball because you are our key player, and you're going to get better and better, and I just assumed you did not play baseball." So I'm the one who really prevented him from playing baseball when he first wanted to in his first year. He didn't complain when I told him. He was on a full scholarship to play basketball and he respected our thinking on that. Tony and I developed a really good relationship in a short period of time. Jim Dietz was the baseball coach back then and Jim is a heckuva guy. Jim approached me the following year and I decided that if Tony really wanted to play baseball, go ahead and play it. That's what happened and the rest is history. He was still a great point guard for us throughout his college career, but baseball is where he wanted to be.

Ted Podleski was the general manager of the San Diego Clippers at that time. Ted has since passed away but later on he was also assistant manager for Jerry Colangelo with the Phoenix Suns. Ted knew basketball very well and we became very good friends over the years when I was in San Diego. He drafted Tony and believed that Tony would have a good chance of making it in the NBA. But he also **DRAFTED HIM LOW***,—tenth round—because he felt Tony was going to go off and play baseball. He thought that's probably what he was going to do or he would have drafted him higher.

I have always felt that Tony could have started for the Clippers. He really loved basketball and had indicated to me that basketball was his most passionate game. Tony tended to put on a little weight and everybody was on his fanny about that, which was ridiculous, but he did. I used to tell him to go play basketball in the off-season and that'll help keep him the weight down. Then he had some issues with his knees, whether it was weight related or not. In fact his local surgeon, Steve Copp, who is now with the Scripps Orthopedic Group in San Diego, played for me at San Diego State for four years. Steve operated on Tony's knees a couple of times and did a lot of surgical repair on Tony's knees.

Tony came off the bench his first year. But he played more minutes as a starter when he was a senior. In fact I recruited another point guard because I wanted to put pressure on Tony. But Tony walked away with the job. Even as a freshman, he was playing more minutes than our starter. He just had a very unique instinct

---

*Bruce Jenner (seventh round) and Carl Lewis (round 10) were **NBA DRAFTEES**, Pat Riley was taken in the NFL 11th round by the Cowboys, Tom Glavine in the NHL fourth round by the L.A. Kings. Carl Lewis was also picked by the Cowboys in Round 12.

for basketball—for any sport in fact. He was phenomenal in his ability to lead a team and his ability to deliver the ball at the right time. His quickness was unbelievable. He was so quick. He was quicker than fast. He was a good shooter and he became a better shooter than when he first began. He would penetrate and dish, as well as having the ability to lay up. As he improved in the game he became a better outside shooter.

> His quickness was unbelievable. He was so quick. He was quicker than fast.

He also stood up to Danny Ainge pretty well for us too, when Danny was at BYU. Tony was a great basketball player.

When Tony played against BYU, we were playing in the downtown arena. We were beating BYU by one point, and had the ball with 12 seconds left on the clock. Tony was bringing the ball up and Danny Ainge was guarding him. Tony went off to his right and Danny jumped in front of him and they gave Tony a charge call. Danny goes to the free-throw line, makes two in a row, and they beat us by one. I remember the emotion Tony had after the game. He felt like he cost the team the game, but he didn't. I said to him, "Tony, it was not you. You had great position. We just got a bad call." But his emotion was really significant because it was such an important game for us at that time. That was also the first year we were in that conference and we came in second.

I am a very emotional guy and it is very hard for me to talk about my players without getting emotional, tears in my eyes and all that kind of stuff. One time, I was giving an award to Kim Goetz, who is an Aztec Hall of Famer, and I was talking and introducing Kim to the audience. Tony was the head baseball coach at San Diego State at the time. All of a sudden I got emotional. I could hardly continue and it was just the way it was because I care so much about these kids. And Tony jumps up out of the first row and he says, "Coach, let me take over from you." So he took over and finished up my speech about

Kim Goetz. That was a very special time for me because Tony went out of his way to stand up next to me. He said, "Coach I know how you are. I know how you feel. Let me give you a break." And he did. It made me feel very good.

Tony loved coaching. He loved his players. That was pretty obvious, he just liked people. He was one of those unique people persons.

In 1996 I was a young reporter at WREX in Rockford, Illinois. It was the Chicago Cubs' home opener against the Padres. The big news was Ryne Sandberg had come out of retirement. While the media mobbed him, I spotted Tony Gwynn doing an interview with one reporter. Tony was talking about the tall infield grass at Wrigley Field, and why Mark Grace was never going to win a batting title because he hits so many ground balls. I interrupted with a question. Tony distinctly informed me that as soon as he was done with this other reporter, he'd answer my questions. That was my first etiquette lesson. When the other reporter was done, Tony gave me his full attention and answered every one of my questions.

—**Troy Hirsch**, Sportscaster, Fox 5, San Diego

We'd go to do an appearance and Tony would turn to me and say, "Just one autograph per person, right?" And I'd nod my head. And then a little boy would come up and put three balls down on the table. And I'd say, "Sorry, just one autograph per person." Then Tony would look at me, and look at the little boy and say, "Don't listen to him. He's not in charge."

—**John Boggs**, Gwynn's longtime agent and business partner

A COACH IS A TEACHER...
WITH A DEATH WISH

JIM DIETZ

Born in Eugene, OR, Jim Dietz served as Head Baseball Coach at San Diego State from 1972 until his retirement in 2002. He was inducted into the American Baseball Coaches Association Hall of Fame in 2002. Among the major league standouts tutored by Dietz at San Diego State are Tony Gwynn and first baseman Mark Grace, who collected the most hits of any major league player in the '90s. Past major league players he has coached include Dave Smith of the Chicago Cubs; Bud Black, the current Padres manager; Mark Williamson of the Baltimore Orioles; Al Newman of the Texas Rangers; and Bobby Meacham of the New York Yankees

The whole Gwynn family, his father, his mother are a very classy family. I was very lucky to have Tony's brother Chris play for me, and his son Anthony Jr. play for me. The best Gwynn of them all might've been Charles, the oldest one. He was playing baseball at Cal State-LA and hurt his knee. The surgery was a tough surgery. Back then, they weren't as sophisticated with surgeries as they are today. He was about 6' 1" and had a great throwing arm, but nobody ever knows about him.

The Gwynns were a very loving family. Very nice people. Very talented baseball people. They had a little alleyway between their house and their neighbor's house that would take you to their backyard. If I wanted to do something or make a decision on Tony that might affect him one way or another, I always tried to find his dad. I would find him at the neighborhood store because he liked to smoke a little bit, but the wife wouldn't let him do it in the house. He'd sneak down to the store on the pretext of getting something, and he would have his smoke down there. He'd always say, "Oh yeah, that's good, that's good."

They would always play a lot in the backyard with a golf-sized Wiffle Ball. There was always some kind of athletic activity among the boys. I think when Chris was at San Diego State he hit for a higher batting average than Tony did. He's working for the **SEATTLE MARINERS*** now.

The way I found Tony Gwynn was through Bobby Meacham. We were in the fall baseball, and getting ready to pick a team. A lot of the kids were trying out and I was short an outfielder. Bobby Meacham came in the office one day and said, "Hey coach, I know where there's a really good hitting outfielder." I said, "Oh great! Where is he?" He said, "He's right here on our campus." I said, "Really." That really intrigued me because we found another kid that way, a kid named Flavio Alfaro who later went on to become the most valuable player on the U.S. Olympic baseball team as a shortstop. He was playing in a softball game and I walked by and I saw this kid at shortstop. He happened to be a Cuban and I decided I would try and talk him into playing baseball.

So Bobby came into my office and started talking to me about this outfielder, and it really intrigued me. I knew he was playing basketball, because Bobby told me that. I went to a basketball game to see him play. He was a really good athlete. He was the point guard, and was probably the best point guard on the Coast in college basketball. He was playing for a coach, a good coach. I didn't really want to upset the apple cart, because I was fairly new at San Diego State and I was trying to build a program.

*During the **SEATTLE MARINERS**' first year in 1977, the distance to the fences was measured in fathoms. A fathom is 6 feet. For instance, whereas one park might have a sign that denotes 360 feet, the Kingdome sign would have the number 60...

I had Bobby get word to Tony about coming by the office and we would talk about it. I had never seen Tony play baseball but his actions on the basketball floor were really good. I really liked Tony from the first time I met him. He was soft-spoken and a real gentleman.

When I met with Tony for the first time, I had Bobby Meacham in my office. I didn't have the basketball coach in the office at that time, because I wasn't sure how good Tony was going to be.

So anyway, I met with Tony and he said, "I've always wanted to play baseball." I said, "Well, here's the deal. Come out in the spring when basketball is over. We'll try to figure this out here. We'll see where you fit in." He said, "Okay, that's great. I've really wanted to play baseball." I said, "Why didn't you come by and see me?" He said, "I was on a basketball scholarship and I didn't want to rock the boat." Which is what I didn't want to do in reverse.

He comes out for baseball, and right away the one thing I notice is that his throwing arm wasn't very strong, because he hadn't been throwing a baseball for a couple of years. He only played Connie Mack baseball during the summer in the Long Beach area. He hadn't been taking ground balls or flyballs in the outfield. I was really worried. I put him in left field because he had a left field kind of arm at that time. He took the batting practice and man, oh man, he had this beautiful swing. I don't think in all the years I coached him we ever talked about hitting much because I just left him alone. From the first time I saw him to the last time I saw him his swing was just unbelievable.

After he had that first spring with us, I could see where he was and what he needed to do. I talked to him one day and I said, "You're probably good enough to play in the **NBA***, but how

*In 1994, the White Sox recalled **MICHAEL JORDAN** from Double-A Birmingham to play against the Cubs in the Mayor's Trophy Game at Wrigley Field. Jordan singled and doubled against the Cubs.

long would your career would be?" I'm sure he had already thought this through, because at 5' 10", he knew in his heart that he'd be better off in baseball because he could hit.

There was only one big decision I had to make with Tony. He went off to play summer ball in Boulder, Colorado where I was the coach. The team was called the Baseline Collegians, and they were a summer powerhouse. I had 23 players on that team, and we played almost every day. About 18 of those guys became major league players off that one summer team. One night, Tony got a base hit and was going to turn it into two, but tripped going around first base. He was on the ground in pain when I ran out to him. I thought, "Oh my God, he broke his foot." I looked at it. It didn't look like a break to me, it looked like a dislocation.

> He went to summer school at the University of Colorado–this is something very few people know.

I had to make a decision. I had them call for an ambulance. I guessed that it was a dislocated ankle instead of a break and I was correct. I manipulated it a bit and pulled down on it and I could feel it pop into place. If we had left it that way they'd probably have to do surgery on it and it would surely hurt his chances in professional baseball. We sent him home for the rest of the summer. There were a lot of things along the way that Tony was either very lucky at or very good at, and one of them is he was lucky his ankle wasn't broken. It was lucky that I had an idea how to pop it in. That's the only ankle I've ever popped in in my life.

He went to summer school at the University of Colorado—this is something very few people know. He spent one summer at the University of Colorado and he'd have to come over to our apartment and do his assignment. He took 10 units which were transferable to San Diego State. My wife was his tutor. She made sure that he was there and that he did his work. It was always fun to see him. He did really well and that was the tipping point for his grades because once he figured out he could do well if he sat down and spent time at it, it turned him around academically.

The only time we talked about hitting in his career was one time the Padres wanted him to hit more home runs. We went to lunch. I said, "Here's the pros and cons as I see it. You could hit more home runs, but you probably wouldn't get on base as much and your batting average wouldn't be what it was." I told him, "If you keep on hitting over .300 every year you'll probably be in the Hall of Fame." He smiled at me and said, "Well, that's a little far-fetched." I said, "No, no. You have a great swing. Stay with that and you'll have success. Now if you lose your success with that swing, then you can try to broaden out and hit a few more home runs. But, you know you're going to have to hit some bad pitches sometimes to hit home runs and I don't think you want to change your strike zone either." Then I left it up to him. He had such success over his first few years that I didn't want to ruin it by giving him advice. I didn't want him to change his swing. People didn't realize that we had that conversation, but we did. He was probably one of the few hitters I've ever had that I never made an adjustment with, 'cause I didn't have to. He was just so fluid.

Jack McKeon used to come to all our practices 'cause Jack's son Casey used to play with us at that time. Of course, by watching his son, he was also watching Tony Gwynn. Then, when it was time for the Padres to draft somebody, Tony was right there.

I didn't think they were going to take Tony as high as they did. When you look at Tony and you look at all the tangibles, he wasn't the tallest guy, he wasn't the fastest guy, and he was still improving as an outfielder. But McKeon saw the same things as I did. I knew Tony was going to go a long way in pro ball.

There are too many things that go on in pro ball that probably shouldn't go on. They're too quick to make suggestions and try to change people. The best thing you can do in pro ball is let somebody show you what they've got and then try to make small adjustments. I think with Jack watching Tony every day for at least three or four months in the fall and then in the spring before he'd have to get back to his duties as manager and general manager, really helped Tony. Tony was really lucky. There were a lot of people in his life who helped him become what he was, and I would have to say that Jack McKeon was one of them. It's just a wonderful thing when you see somebody, and you know they're talented, and then it works out because it doesn't always work out that way. Things happen.

With Tony, I knew he wasn't going to do anything bad off the field. He was one of those athletes that if he had success you'd never know about it or if he had failure you wouldn't know about it because he never let that affect him one way or the other. A slump for him was going hitless maybe in one or two games in a row, and that was a big slump. He didn't change a thing. He toyed with it a little when the Padres first talked to him about trying to hit more **HOME RUNS***.

The biggest improvement that Tony made in our program and in his career was not in his hitting but in how he became a really good defensive outfielder. He went from being somebody who had a very average throwing arm, to somebody who knew how to throw, how to use the spin turn in the outfield. He played in right field later on which is a difficult position to play in the outfield. Of course, he threw left-handed and that helped him because he didn't have to make many spin turns to make a throw to second base or hit the cutoff man.

When he played pro ball, he would also always come back to San Diego State in the fall. In the fall, Tony concentrated on his defense. He would take fly ball after fly ball as my assistant coaches would hit as many fly balls as he wanted. Then when

---

*Rod Carew once led the American League in batting average without hitting a **HOME RUN**.

we were taking live batting practice, he wanted to play shallow in the outfield so he would have to work on going back and being in proper throwing position. He didn't throw a lot in the fall but he certainly worked on getting his feet in position, and lining up fly balls and working on ground balls in the outfield, because a lot of times with a ground ball the guy on second base is going to try and score. He was always working to get in the proper position to make strong throws. By doing that, his arm strength got better, his throwing got better, and his fielding got better. Tony thought that it was more important to do that in the fall than in spring.

It's one of these things where Tony was always at the right place, at the right time, and the right people could see him. So much of that is true for the guys who get that opportunity, but the nice thing about Tony is that he could pull it off. Tony was never in awe of anything. Nothing really bothered him much. Seeing a really good **MAJOR-LEAGUE PITCHER*** was never a problem for Tony. The bigger the name the more he stayed inside the ball and the harder he hit it through the hole. I don't remember him ever having to bunt for a base hit.

He reminds me a lot of Rod Carew, because Rod would get base hit after base hit, and so would Tony. Rod told me that he was a firm believer that you had to have a flat spot in your swing to support contact. With a round ball and a round bat you need that three or four inches where the bat is flat to support contact and hit the ball hard. Maybe you won't hit a lot of home runs,

*In 1971, Ted Williams wrote a book called *The Science of Hitting*. Gwynn first read it when he was at San Diego State and read it two or three times each year when he was a Major League player. Gwynn would highlight passages, he would fill the margins with notes, and he loved the cover, which showed the strike zone filled with baseballs, each ball with an average attached. The balls represented Williams' estimate of a batter's stats if he hit **PITCHES** only in that area. Gwynn committed the zone to memory.

but you'll get a lot of base hits. Tony reminds me of that kind of hitter because he always had a flat spot in his swing.

I just feel very fortunate to have had a relationship with the Gwynn family. Tony is just one of those career athletes that there's nothing bad that can be said about him, his brothers, or his family. They are just a first-class family, first-class people. You would never know that he was a Hall of Fame baseball player. You'd never know that he won all those batting crowns, Gold Gloves, and things. If you didn't know who he was, you'd never know he was a baseball player. He would never talk about himself. He would never put himself out there. I was very fortunate to be there and be involved with his development.

> **He would never talk about himself.**

Of course it started with his mom and dad. His dad was a real crack up. I really enjoyed him. His mom was real quiet, but you always had the feeling you had to pass muster with her. She was always looking out for her boys. I miss seeing Charles and Anthony. I was at the service for Tony and I saw Anthony. He has really gotten taller now and filled out. Chris looks so much like Tony except he's maybe an inch or two taller.

Temperament can ruin your career. If you try too hard, you're going to fail. If you don't try hard enough, you're going to fail. If you think you're great, you're going to fail. If you think you're no good, you're going to fail. You have to have that right temperament. That's something that the scouts don't really look for enough. The right temperament is critical in the development of an athlete especially in baseball because there's so much failure. To hit .300 means you're failing 70 percent of the time. So you have to be able to deal with that. Tony had that great makeup. So did Chris, his brother. .

KNOWING TONY GWYNN WAS LIKE PLAYING HOOKY FROM LIFE

JOHN MAFFEI

A 1971 graduate of San Diego State, John Maffei lettered in baseball for the Aztecs. His first job was as a sportswriter at the Escondido Times-Advocate. *He returned to San Diego State as Sports Information Director in 1972 and held that position through the 1978 season when he returned to the* Times-Advocate *as sports editor. He moved to the* Oceanside Blade-Tribune *as a sportswriter in 1985, then was part of the merger when the* Times-Advocate *and* Blade-Tribune *joined forces to form the* North County Times. *He joined the U-T San Diego staff in 2012. He has covered all sports from preps to pros.*

I was the Sports Information Director at San Diego State when Tony was there as a basketball and baseball player. I had played baseball at San Diego State prior to Tony getting there, and then had taken a newspaper job. But a year after taking the newspaper job I was hired back at San Diego State as Sports Information Director. I was 22 years old and the youngest sports information director in the country at that time. I was young enough to still be a player. The first contact I had with Tony and Alicia was when he stopped by my office and said, "I'm Tony Gwynn. I'm trying to find the basketball office." This was when he was coming out of high school, and I had heard the coaches talking about this Tony Gwynn kid.

Now, the summer before, Vince Ferragamo who was a great quarterback at Cal, had come by and poked his head into my office. I tried feverishly to find a coach, because Vince Ferragamos don't walk into your office every day. Not only was he handsome, but I thought, "This is a football player." He was looking to transfer to San Diego State before he went to Nebraska. I was scrambling like a big dog trying to find a coach. This was July and the coaches either weren't around or they had gone home early. I was making phone calls trying to get coaches at home who could get back to the campus. I finally found Ted Tollner at home, and I said, "Vince Ferragamo is in my office." He said to me, "Would you stop it. It's Friday, it's five o'clock. Go home. Don't do this." I said, "Vince Ferragamo is in the office." He said, "John, I've had 4 or 5 beers." I said, "I don't care what you had. You're the first guy that answered his phone. You've got to get here." We didn't get Ferragamo, but it wasn't because we didn't try.

> "I knew you when your hair was this big," holding my hands way out, "and when your butt was this big," holding them real close.

I wasn't going to let that happen again. I wasn't going to let Tony Gwynn walk around campus by himself. The basketball office was just down the hall. I introduced myself and said, "Tony, I'm going to walk you down to the coach's office." The basketball coach's door was open, but nobody was there. I knew that if the coaches' door was open, they're around. If it's closed, they're not around. We walked around, poked our heads into a couple of offices, and sure enough we found the coach and Tony ends up coming to San Diego State.

That was the start of a great relationship. We were both base-ball players. Obviously, he was a lot better than me but our ages were not that far off. He was a slight kind of kid with a big Afro. It's funny, because years later when the writers were get-ting on him about his weight—by this time I had transitioned to be a sportswriter—he claimed that he was the same weight that he was when he was at San Diego State. I was in the back of the room and I just went, "Bull - - - -." And he goes, "Who is that?" I said, "I knew you when your hair was this big," holding my hands way out, "and when your butt was this big," holding them real close. "Now your hair is this big and your butt is this big." He just cracked up. He said, "That's why I like you. You're the only guy who will speak up and say it like it is. You don't beat around the bush."

I've been 50 years in the business now and people ask me, "What's your favorite moment in sports?" Well, Tony used to always take batting practice about 2 o'clock before everyone else came out. As beat writers, we knew that, and would come out and watch Tony hit. When he was finished, we would just sit there on the bench and talk sports with him while everybody else was taking batting practice. He just loved to talk sports with us. When the Padres were playing the Yankees in the World Series I got to **YANKEE STADIUM*** really early on a workout day. There was hardly anybody there, so I decided it would be a good time to walk around Monument Park to see the monuments. I was there all by myself thinking this was unbelievable. I felt a hand on my shoulder and I turned around. It was Tony. I said, "What are you doing out here?" He said, "I'm doing the same thing you're doing. I'm looking at the monuments." Two guys had the same idea to go out and look at the monuments while nobody else was around.

Tony had a great understanding about the history of the game and great respect for it. He knew who the greats were and where they grew up. He grew up as a Dodger fan and had a great appreciation of the great Dodger players. And not just baseball. He loved football and would follow the football team at San Diego State. He loved the Indiana Pacers. At that time Alicia had a Christian music recording studio in Indianapolis. He would drive her back there. While Alicia was busy in the studio, Tony bought Pacers season tickets so that he would have something to do when he was there.

---

* The cement used to build **YANKEE STADIUM** was purchased from Thomas Edison who owned the huge Portland Cement Company.

He loved basketball. His son Anthony went to Poway High and played basketball there. In his sophomore year, Garry Templeton, Jr. and Anthony were the guards and they had two seven-footers on the team. They walked the ball up the floor and passed the ball to the big guys. At the end of the season, Garry and Anthony wanted to transfer out because they didn't want to walk the ball up the floor. But Tony was adamant. He said, "You go to the high school where you live." They lived right behind Poway High. Anthony could walk to the school. They sat down with the coach and they asked, "What are you thinking?" He said, "I had two seven-footers last year. What am I going to do? We were going to walk the ball and pound it in. Now, what do I have? I've got six-four, six-five guys and two racehorse guards. What am I going to do? We're going to fly, guys. We're going to get the ball and we're going to go. I'm going to turn you guys loose." Tony just looked at Anthony and said, "What did I tell you? You're staying here. You're loyal to the school where you're at. You don't transfer when things get tough."

Anthony was a very good basketball player, and Tony would film every game. He would arrive late for the game and would get there right before tipoff with his video camera. Then he'd go right up in the stands so that he could film every one of Anthony's games. Sometimes people would bother him for autographs, and his only rule was. "Don't bother me during the game. I'll sign anything for you afterwards. Bring your stuff up after the game and I'll stay as late as it takes to take care of everyone. Please don't bother me while I'm trying to watch my son." They would make an announcement letting people know that.

When you looked at his autograph you could tell that is was Tony Gwynn. One time at San Diego State the athletic director was trying to drop the baseball program. The coach and I were close, so we got Tony and held one of those autograph-card show kind of deals on the field. We raised about $50,000 that day and Tony was signing autographs for $5 apiece, which was nuts because we should've charged more. He was carefully signing his name as usual, and I said to him, "Why do you do that? Why don't you scribble your name like everybody else does?" He goes, "Because that might be the only time that person, whether it's a man, woman, or child, has the opportunity to meet a major-league player. I want that person to get my full attention, walk away, and if I'm the only major leaguer he ever meets I want him to think that I'm a good guy. It doesn't take me 10 seconds to write the signature that people can read. If they're paying for an autograph show or if they're paying to go to a game and wait for me outside afterwards, I owe them the courtesy of giving them a legible signature."

> "If they're paying for an autograph... I owe them the courtesy of giving them a legible signature."

Basketball coach Smokey Gaines called Tony Gwynn 'the black Pillsbury Doughboy.' Tim Vezie, Tony's basketball coach his freshman year, was a good coach and a good guy. Tim surrounded himself with really good coaches. Tim was a really good practice coach and prepared the guys well. But then they brought in Smokey. Tony confided in me that he had always wanted to play for a black coach. Then. when he started playing for Smokey, he said, "Boy, you got to be careful what you wish for. I learned a lot. The color of your skin doesn't matter. If you're a good guy you're a good guy, but if you're a jerk, you're a jerk."

Tony loved basketball. He and I talked about his decision to be a baseball player rather than a basketball player. He told me that when he sat down and thought about it he realized that he was a five-foot, ten-inch point guard and that he was not going to be a great scorer in the NBA. He said, "I can pass and I can do some things but when you sit down and look at my record, I could probably get 3 to 5 years out of this body in the NBA. In baseball, if I'm as good as people are telling me I am, I might be able to get 10 to 12 years out of this in the major leagues." As a matter of longevity he chose baseball because he thought he could have a longer career.

Bob Cluck was a scout with the Astros when Tony was a junior. Bob had pitched at San Diego State, lived in San Diego, and was very familiar with the program. He wanted the Astros to pick Tony in the first round, but the Astros didn't have a first- or second-round draft pick that year. So, first round goes and Tony's not taken, second round goes and Tony's not taken. In the third round, the Padres are picking two picks before the Astros. Jack McKeon was in the draft room and he said, "If you don't pick Tony Gwynn all of you are fired." The scouts were telling McKeon that Tony would be there in the fourth round but Jack knew that the Astros were going to take him in the that round. He told them, "Cluck is going to take him. If we don't take Tony in the third round he's gone." Jack had scouted the players at San Diego State. Bob Cluck was crushed because he had put a lot of effort into trying to get Tony but Jack McKeon ended up stealing him from him. Jack was pretty observant and when you're scouting San Diego State and you see Bob Cluck there enough, he's not there just to scout Bobby Meacham. He's looking at more than one guy. So Jack knew that Tony wasn't going to last much longer and that they'd better take him in the third round.

> Jack McKeon was in the draft room and he said, "If you don't pick Tony Gwynn all of you are fired."

Tony gave me a hard time when I left the job as Sports Information Director at San Diego State to become a news reporter. He said, "You were one of us and now you're one of them."

Tony was a dipper. He put the tobacco in his front lip. He was never a leaf tobacco guy. The SDSU coaching staff would not let you have tobacco, so it had to be when he got to the minor leagues when it started.

Tim Zier was one of his recruits. Tony called me about him and said, "I think I want this Zier kid." I told Tony that Tim Zier was a throwback to the Jim Dietz era. "Tim Zier will take a ball off his face. He'll spit his teeth out, throw you out at first, and then go back and pick his teeth up." Tony goes, "I got to have that kid." Zier had a great year as a junior but didn't get drafted. Tony's advice to Tim was, "Hey, listen kid, take it out on the baseball field. Take it out on every opponent this season and make them pay. Then you'll get drafted and you'll get a chance."

He did not die from the cancer, he died of a heart attack. The official cause of death was heart failure. Tony was diabetic and my understanding is that between the medicine for diabetes and the chemo and everything for cancer, it was too much for him. His heart just gave out. He died that night after Father's Day, early on Monday morning. He had had a very good day on Sunday. He was very upbeat. Anthony was playing for the Phillies in a home game on Sunday and then flew to Atlanta with the Phillies. Tony was having a good day—he was not at death's door. Otherwise, Anthony would've flown home. He would not have flown to Atlanta. And Tony's brother, Chris who works for the Mariners, would have flown to San Diego to be with Alicia and the family. Nobody knew it was imminent because they would have gathered.

Alicia was a high school sprinter. Her brother, Mickey Cureton, was one of the legendary high school football players in the Los Angeles area and went to UCLA, where he was a star running back. Alicia was a sprinter at San Diego State. I asked her one day why she talked to me and not a lot of other people. She said it was because I was really nice to them when they were just Tony and Alicia before they were married, and that I had always treated them like decent people. She told me that a lot of people started treating them special once Tony became successful in the major leagues.

One of the writers had wanted to do a story about Anthony Jr. so I hooked them up. The writer called me back afterwards and said, "I never thought I'd ever interview anybody that was nicer than Tony Gwynn. But after talking to Anthony, I think it's a tie." That's the nicest compliment I heard about Tony.

My lasting memory of Tony is that he was an absolutely salt of the earth guy. I can't imagine that there will ever be another one.

BAY WATCH

RICK BAY

Rick Bay enjoyed a 25-year career as a sports executive beginning at the University of Oregon where he was Athletic Director. That job was followed by positions as Athletic Director at the Ohio State University, Chief Operating Officer of the New York Yankees, Athletic Director at the University of Minnesota, President of the Cleveland Indians, and Athletic Director at San Diego State University. At SDSU, he hired Steve Fisher as the basketball coach and Tony Gwynn as head baseball coach. He is also author of Have Resume, Will Travel: My Nomadic Life as a Sports Executive. *Bay graduated from the University of Michigan and has retired to Ann Arbor and Palm Desert, CA.*

It's a very difficult job. When I went to San Diego State, they were on the verge of dropping football and simply becoming a Division 3 school. We fought tooth and nail to keep Division 1 sports a part of San Diego State. If there was one sport that was played more consistently over a long period of time it was San Diego State baseball. San Diego State football was hurting, and they had just hired Ted Tollner when I arrived.

I got to know Tony once I became Athletic Director. I had wanted to improve the athletic facilities at San Diego State. They were awful. We had a baseball stadium at the time, if you can call it a stadium... I call it the park. It was put together—using Band-Aids almost—through the ingenuity of Coach Dietz, who had kept the program alive for a long time, and had many winning seasons.

I knew we needed to do something to inject some spark into the program. One of the things I thought we could do right off the bat, because it was affordable if I could get the money, was build a new baseball park.

The new owner of the San Diego Padres was a guy by the name of John Moores. I didn't know him at all, but he was trying to do good things for the Padres, and I was trying to do good things for the Aztecs. I thought my best strategy, even though I didn't know John Moores, was to see if he might be interested in making a major contribution to San Diego State Athletics, to go toward building a new baseball stadium, and to name it Tony Gwynn Stadium.

> "Rick, you're going to need a lot more than a million dollars to fix this dump up."

I knew he had been really generous when he lived in Houston. He had helped the University of Houston athletic program stay alive. The athletic director at Houston called me when John had bought the Padres and said "There's a guy in your community now who can really help you, if he wants to."

I went to see John, and said "John, you don't know me at all, and I have no right to ask you this, but I have an idea that could help both of us and honor your most valuable player at the same time, and that would be if you would give me a million dollars to build a new ballpark on the campus and name it Tony Gwynn Stadium.

John said, "Well, let me come out and see what you have." He came out a few days later, and he walked into our park, and looked around, and said, "Rick, you're going to need a lot more than a million dollars to fix this dump up." He ended up giving us about five million dollars to build the ballpark.

We named it Tony Gwynn Stadium, even though, to Tony's credit, he thought it should be named after his own coach, Jim Dietz, who was still the baseball coach at the time.

Jim Dietz was ready to retire. We were winning more games than we were losing, but we were not taking that next step in NCAA regional play, and certainly we had never been to the College World Series. I was about to embark on a search for a new coach. Tony's son, Anthony Jr., was playing on the team at the time for Coach Dietz, and he was destined to be drafted by a Major League team soon.

Tony decided to let it be known to me that he would like to be the new coach. He had opportunities to go into broadcasting and other things, which he did on a part-time basis. But once he let it be known that he wanted to be a candidate for the job, and he was really respectful about how he did it—I want to emphasize that—once he let it be known, then nobody else even applied.

There were several good college baseball coaches in California, guys that had gone to the College World Series—Cal State-Northridge, Cal State-Irvine, and a couple of others—that I would have liked to have interviewed. But once Tony was a public candidate, nobody else was going to even interview for the job. There was no way I could not hire Tony Gwynn in San Diego. On top of that, other potential candidates didn't want to be losers in a job search that was a loser proposition to begin with.

But I did have to go through all the University and state rigmarole. I had to post the job and agree to at least examine the credentials if not interview anybody who applied through the state system. Nobody else did apply, but I had to go through the formality of interviewing Tony. To Tony's credit, when the day of the interview came, even though he knew I had no other alternative, he still showed up at my office with a coat and tie, and we went through the formal interview process.

I asked him the kind of questions that I would ask any candidate, plus questions that I wasn't sure he was really prepared to answer, such as, how was he going to counsel his student athletes on academic matters, what would his training regimen be, what was his philosophy on scheduling, all of those kinds of the philosophical things that any candidate would have to answer. Tony did his best to answer them, and did them quite satisfactorily. We shook hands and I hired him. I could only pay him $100,000 as salary. The Padres paid him at least ten times that much just to walk around the stadium after he retired just to shake hands with people.

He also was doing some part-time work with ESPN, and that became a little bit of an issue with other college coaches who thought that San Diego State would have this recruiting advantage if Tony talked up the Aztecs on a national broadcast. So it was agreed by all—Tony, the NCAA, San Diego State, and other coaches—that Tony being named our new coach would not be mentioned on the air. And it wasn't.

My biggest concern with Tony was that he didn't have any coaching experience, and that may seem a trifle, but I have seen a lot of great athletes who couldn't coach a lick. I mean, they couldn't tell you what they did to achieve what they achieved. They couldn't break down their mechanics. They just did what they did naturally. I've seen a lot of great coaches who couldn't play a lick. It goes both ways, but playing and coaching are different skill sets.

> I have seen a lot of great athletes who couldn't coach a lick.

I was concerned that he had no experience in coaching, and secondly, the Padres were still paying him something in a public relations role, and ESPN was still using him on broadcasts. Every coach that I ever had in any sport, was contributing a hundred percent of his energy and time to just coaching. I was worried that Tony might spread himself too thin and not be as focused on coaching as some of the people he was coaching against.

I also knew that he had some great advantages. Every baseball player knew who he was. He could get his foot in any great high school baseball player's door, no matter what, which couldn't be said of most other coaches because they didn't have the credentials. That was a terrific advantage. I also told Tony that fame is fleeting, and that once he got four or five years into his coaching career, what he had done as a player would begin to fade, and he would have to be able to recruit based on his coaching record, not his playing record.

We also decided that if this worked out to everyone's advantage, that we would have Jim Dietz stay on one additional year, and have Tony serve as his assistant....his volunteer assistant in the dugout for a year, to get a feel for what it was to coach a college baseball team. That would make it easier for him to transition into the head job a year later when Coach Dietz left.

I knew he used tobacco, and it's against the rules in intercollegiate baseball to use at practice or during games. I didn't try to lecture him on any of that, but I knew that he had tried to get away from it a couple of times without any success.

I didn't know Tony, Jr. very well. He was just one of those student-athletes. A very nice young man, well mannered. I knew him like I knew the other kids on the team. They knew who I was. There's sort of an odd relationship between student athletes and athletic administrators. They don't know quite what to make of all the "suits" who walk around the complex. If Tony, Jr. went by me, he would call me "Mr. Bay," and move along. Of course I went to a lot of the games, so they knew who I was, and Tony's wife and their daughters were there all the time too. They are a great family.

SWEET HOME, SAN DIEGO STATE

KIRK KENNEY

Kirk Kenney joined the Union-Tribune in 1985, shortly after graduating from San Diego State, where he majored in business (real estate) and minored in journalism. He was born in Escondido and raised in La Mesa, where he attended Helix High School in the post-Bill Walton and pre-Reggie Bush era, and now lives in the North County community of Santaluz. Kirk has covered everything from the preps to the pros through the years.

He really had really rock star status. Everywhere he went with his SDSU team, the team drew great big crowds. But the crowds were more to see Tony Gwynn, and maybe get his autograph, than to see the team. It took a while for him to try and get the focus back on his players. But he was always very accommodating just like he was when he was a player 'cause he didn't want to turn people away. He thought also that maybe if people came out to see him, that they would also see his team and his players, and come away thinking more about college baseball, and maybe want to come back.

When he first started as a coach, he had a lot of learning to do. Most college baseball coaches got into it at a young age, and learned coming up as assistants before getting their first chance to become a head coach. Obviously, he knew the game as well as or better than anybody.

He's biggest adjustment was getting to learn about guiding and teaching eighteen to twenty-one year olds. Also, some of the other aspects of the game, like recruiting. The first couple of years, he recruited very, very well. But, they recruited too well, because they had guys that would be first-round draft picks or second-round draft picks that ended up signing with Major League Baseball rather than going to college. So they had to learn how to get the second-tier guys as well. He wasn't able to get a lot of high-profile commitments. His name brought people out who wanted to check out the campus and consider San Diego State, 'cause everyone was eager to be coached by Tony Gwynn.

One other thing that people don't consider is that Tony Gwynn added something to the entire campus and community of San Diego State, not just the baseball program. When **PETCO PARK*** opened in 2004, he called its chairman, and arranged for San Diego State to play the first games played at the new park. San Diego State played the first game there against Houston, which was to honor Padres owner John Moores' alma mater, and the Aztecs shut them out. That brought one million dollars to the San Diego State athletics program. He was always very proud of the donation they were able to get, and also being able to put on an event like that for college baseball. That also was the largest crowd ever in college baseball history. Just over 40,000 people showed up. That's still the college baseball record, and he was also very proud of that.

The atmosphere that night was just electric. Everybody was so eager to see the new Petco Park downtown and to be able to have a college tournament there made it all the more special for the players. You could see Tony just beaming with pride at being able to show off what the big leagues are all about to his players. The combination of that, and also to have the largest

*Other than Tony Gwynn, Mark Loretta is the only Padre to crack the top ten in hitting. Loretta is 10th on the all-time hitting list. Loretta also hit the first home run at **PETCO PARK** in 2004, after being the last Padre to homer in Qualcomm Stadium in 2003.

crowd ever in baseball history, and to then go ahead and win the game, made everything just a perfect evening.

Gwynn might get frustrated if players struck out or didn't execute but no more so than any other coach would. Especially when he was sick, you could tell how beloved he was by the players, and how much they missed him when he was away dealing with his illness.

He was getting better and better as a coach as he went on. Early on, he had a lot to learn, because for twenty years all he had to do was worry about how to be the best player he could be. After that it was more about how to be a good coach, and teaching players how to execute and achieve. It's funny 'cause a lot of things he was teaching were more like a 501 class rather than a 101 class. A lot of players would come back after going on to pro ball. That's when it really clicked for them, some of the things he was trying to teach. They used to say it takes a certain amount of at-bats for it to finally make sense and sink in.

San Diego State was really getting things turned around in the right direction. His last two seasons they made the NCAA tournament. They also made the tournament in 2009 when they had Stephen Strasburg. Strasburg was a very down-to-earth, shy, and very private person. Tony's presence was invaluable to him, because Tony had been through so much of that fame and fortune. Tony knew what was coming for Stephen and he was able to talk him through a lot of that. That made the road ahead for Stephen Strasburg much easier than it might have been had there not been someone of Tony Gwynn's stature there for him.

There were a couple of times when Tony Gwynn came out and argued with the umpires. He got ejected a couple of times, although I think every time he was ejected he was actually in the right. The first time, he got ejected because the ump said he had the wrong jacket on and it turned out the umpire was wrong. That particular year, they were being real strict about the uniforms. Some umpire just got it into his head that Gwynn was wearing the wrong thing and for whatever reason decided that was the time to eject him.

As far as on the field game X's and O's, Tony would rank right up with any other **COLLEGE COACHES*** out there.

He wanted to spend as much time with his players as he could, and you could tell even when he was feeling really, really badly he would be out there. He did in fact tell me that being around his players was what kept him going.

I don't think the players ever realized that he might not come back, because the hope was that he was always coming back. Even the week before he died, the school had given him a contract extension....

I stopped in on Tony unannounced one day at San Diego State. He was collecting all this stuff. He had some Padres jerseys and balls and other memorabilia, some Aztecs gear, and he was signing all of it. He was putting together a memorabilia goody bag. I said, "What's all that stuff for?"

He goes on to tell me how he met this woman at an autograph signing in Iowa. She told Tony how she had grown up in San Diego, and moved to **IOWA***, but she's a lifelong Padres fan, and she can't wait to get back to get back to town to go on a tour of Petco Park, 'cause she hadn't been in town since it opened.

Tony gives her a throwaway comment. "When you get into town look me up and I'll give you a tour." It's one of those things

---

*In 2003, Tony Gwynn was the Mountain West Conference **COACH** of the Year.

---

* The only stadium named for a Heisman Trophy winner is Nile Kinnick Stadium at the University of **IOWA**. Nile Kinnick was Bob Feller's catcher in American Legion ball. Kinnick was killed in WWII when his plane was shot down....In 1974, the Padres had a pitcher from an unlikely named Iowa town. Jim McAndrew was from Lost Nation, Iowa.

you say. But about six months later he gets a phone call from that woman and she says "Hey, we're in town and we're ready for that tour." He was caught off guard because he had practice that day but you could tell he felt so obligated because he had made that statement that he was putting all this together. I rode down with him to give it to her, and of course she knows nothing about this. We get out of the car and her tour group was right there, just about to go on the tour.

All of a sudden she sees him, and she's just totally overwhelmed. She doesn't know what to do. She can't control her emotions, she hugs him, and she's just beside herself.

Tony said, "I'm sorry. I've got practice and some obligations. I can't take you on the tour, but I got this for you." For this woman and for everyone watching it's a moment they'll never forget and they'll talk about for the rest of their lives.

One of the things in the last few months, the last time I talked to him, I said, "I really want to see you get better 'cause I have a lot of questions about if you would have batted .400." In the past, he has said that he thinks he would have, but I never got the chance to ask those questions. Then I came to realize, you know what, he was going to be gone too soon, no matter what, because I will always have more questions for Tony Gwynn. There always would've been more questions.

There are certain people in life that people really gravitate to, and I think Tony Gwynn had the greatest gravitational pull of anyone I've ever seen. It starts from his greatness on the field, obviously all the batting titles and everything that he accomplished that will join all the greats. But it was more than that, because he stayed in San Diego for 20 years.

He just loved talking baseball. He could meet somebody for five minutes and you'd think they'd been best friends for years. He just enjoyed talking baseball. And then that would lead into other discussions about all kinds of things.

A ROOMIE WITH A VIEW

KEN DAVIS

A lifelong friendship was accidentally formed in 1980 when two San Diego State students were looking for room-mates. Oregonian Ken Davis was paired with Tony Gwynn by SDSU baseball coach Jim Dietz....For several decades, Ken Davis has run a very successful real estate company in San Diego.

Tony being easy to get along with and being a great guy, we hit it off immediately. Our typical nights were playing cards, watching *SportsCenter,* and Tony talking to Alicia on the phone, because she lived in Long Beach at the time. She had gone to San Diego State, graduated, and moved back to Long Beach. They were engaged, so he talked to her every night. He'd sit on the phone with her, play cards, and watch *SportsCenter*. Tony had the most amazing ability to seemingly concentrate on multiple things at the same time.

Guys used to tease him, because when we would get together at some of the other players' houses, Tony would always have to stop and make a call to Alicia. The guys would give him a hard time about it, but he wouldn't go through the evening without talking to Alicia. Alicia's brothers told me a story one time about how her dad would not let boys come into the house to visit her. Boys would come over to the house who wanted to date her, and he refused to let any boys into the house. Then, one day, Tony Gwynn showed up at the door. The Gwynns had such a good reputation in the area. Alicia's father said, "Oh! That's one of the Gwynn boys. Well, the Gwynns are good stock." So, Tony Gwynn was the first boy Alicia's dad ever let into the house to visit with Alicia. He actually got through the front door. All the other guys had to stand at the door and Alicia could talk to them through the front door.

I first met Alicia when she would come down and visit Tony on weekends. Our senior year she worked at a grocery store up in Long Beach and she would bring us different food items that they were going to discard. We had no money. She would bring us food and she would cook for us on the weekends. They met when they were kids and they started dating when he was 14 and she was 15. They were a pair.

> Tony Gwynn was the first boy Alicia's dad ever let into the house to visit with Alicia.

There is no question that Alicia was the right person for Tony.

I wish there was more video out there of him playing basketball because he really was good. He was a Magic Johnson-style of player, obviously much shorter. He had a total court awareness, he knew where everybody was on the floor, and he had the ability to make great passes. He was drafted by the Clippers on the same day as he was drafted by the Padres. He asked the Padres if he could try out for the Clippers. There was no hope of course, but he really wanted to. He was pretty confident that he could make the team. He didn't know if he could be a starter but he wanted to give it a shot. He pushed the Padres on it, and obviously they said, "You're either a baseball player at this stage or a basketball player. You're not going to be both professionally." So he didn't get to pursue that dream.

I'm from Eugene, Oregon. I spent the summer there so I got to see him a few times his first year in the minors, when he played in Walla Walla. When he came to play in Eugene, he stayed at my folks' house instead of at the team motel for a few nights. My dad was a homicide detective up in Eugene at that time. He took Tony to lunch one day when Walla Walla played in Eugene. When he was driving back, he asked Tony to stay in the car when they got to the motel where the team was staying. My dad went out and showed his badge to some of the guys on the team, pointed at Tony in the car and said, "Hey, do you know this guy? I just arrested him." He was trying to play a joke. All the guys started laughing and told him that it couldn't be Tony. The joke didn't work because all the guys knew that Tony was too good of a guy to get in trouble. They knew it was some kind of a setup.

About that time, the Padres were going to bring Tony up to Double-A Amarillo. Also at that time was the Northwest League All-Star Game, so the Padres put off bringing him up for a few days so that he could play in that game. He ended up playing first base, which was absolutely crazy because they had too many out-fielders and not enough infielders. Typical minor league deal!

The next day he was going to fly out to Amarillo. Tony didn't show his emotions a lot. But that morning he was a combination of nervousness and excitement about moving up to AA. He knew he was ready for a higher level of baseball. Tony was real confident pretty much all the time. We got to the airport in what I thought was plenty of time, but there was a long line. Tony was concerned that he'd miss the flight. He said to me, "I don't want to miss this flight. This is a big opportunity for me. I can't miss this flight." I was sweating bullets thinking, "Man, if he misses this flight, it's my fault." Well, he made the flight, and the rest is history. He hit the heck out of the ball in Amarillo....

One time at San Diego State, we were getting ready for a game against a pitcher that was supposed to be real good. I said to Tony, "I don't know about this. This guy is really good. It's going to be a tough day." Tony said to me, "Well if you think he's better than you, why bother going up to the plate?" That was the way he was. He was not demonstrative or cocky on the field, but he had a quiet confidence in his abilities. He knew that he could handle things. That was the way he was with everything. He wouldn't show a lot of excitement if things went well.

One time, when Tony had been with the Padres for years, I was down in the clubhouse with him and we walked out from the clubhouse to the field. As we walked out to the field, we saw the team president pass us. The big shot said, "Hey Tony, how're you doing?" Tony thought he was an arrogant jerk. As we reached the field, the groundskeeper guys were getting ready to go work on the field. As soon as Tony saw them, his face lit up. He asked, "How did it go? How did the game go?" He knew that the groundskeepers had a softball team. The Padres had just gotten back in town, so Tony didn't know how their playoff game had gone. He spent 10 minutes laughing and joking with these guys, kidding them and asking them about their softball league. That's the epitome of Tony. He didn't care who somebody was as far as their position in life or their perceived status.

He would not use his position in any way to gain favor with people. Tony loved talking to people who were not impressed by him. He would be uncomfortable with people who were in awe of him. When people would go, "Oh, it's Tony Gwynn. Oh, I love you. You're the greatest," he would just smile and thank them. Then he'd look at me and roll his eyes. But, when we'd run into someone who'd talk to him about cars or something else, he'd talk with them all day. He'd be happy to talk baseball as long as they weren't putting him on a pedestal. He'd have a great time, laugh, and tell stories.

Tony did not like arrogant people. He did a promotion with a big-name player in the early '90s. The big star was treating people like dirt because he wasn't getting the attention he thought he deserved. He kept saying, "I'm the talent here. I'm the talent. You guys need to start serving me. I'm not here to serve you." Tony said, "I about walked off. I couldn't take it. All these people there trying to do the best they can and make this thing happen for us. We're getting paid for it and he has to strut around like he's some big-time somebody." Tony didn't care for that at all.

Tony never felt like he was special other than he knew he had a special talent. But he didn't think that made him any better than anybody. They had a lot of ceremonies for him over the years, but Tony really didn't like being the center of attention.

For him it was more about helping out the Padres rather than to bring attention to himself. Tony would complain to me that when the Padres wanted to do a public service announcement they always came to him because all the other guys wouldn't do it. The Padres could rely on him. So not only was he the star of the team, but he was the guy they could depend when they needed to do some public relations type of a deal.

> Jay Leno asked him to come on his show several times over the years...

Tony went out of his way for a lot of people and never asked for anything in return. People who worked for the Padres, some of the announcers and some of the other people who worked there, who had kids in school would ask him to talk their kids' class. Tony would do it without ever telling the Padres because he knew it would get him in trouble. In fact, one time, there was a school in New York—this was 15 or 20 years ago—it was in a poor, ghetto type of area. They had all kinds of trouble with the kids. Tony met somebody who asked if he would speak to the kids. It ended up the only time he could do it was in the off-season. Tony, at his own expense, flew to New York, talked to the kids, and flew back to San Diego all in the same day. That's a huge trip to make just for somebody he didn't really know other than to know that they were associated with the school. He just thought it was the right thing to do.

Jay Leno asked him to come on his show several times over the years and Tony always turned it down. I said, "Tony, why don't you go on the show?" He said, "I didn't make a movie. I'm not promoting anything. I don't have anything to sell. Why would I go on the show?" I don't know anybody else who would come up with that excuse. I just thought if you're invited to go on the Jay Leno show you go on. It's just something you do.

I had to pull teeth to get him to tell me about dinner at the White House with George Bush. In fact, I had to go to Alicia to find out some details about how the whole thing went. Before they went he told me "Alicia really wants to go, so we're going to go. I know it's cool. Meet the President, see the White House, but that's a long trip to make just to have a dinner and then fly back." But Alicia said, "It's the White House, it's the President. We're going." Tony was the most down to earth person and the least impressed by somebody's position or wealth or fame of anyone I know.

Tony was never a phony. And he said controversial things. During the steroids thing, he came out and said pretty much what was on his mind.

I played a lot of golf with Tony. He wasn't the best golfer out there and neither am I. Generally we would go out at the end of the day after the last foursome had left, and we would play until it was dark. He enjoyed that because there was nobody watching him and we could play at our own pace. We could play, shoot the breeze and take our time. Tony had 'Tony Gwynn' golf balls—they had his signature on them. He would never let me use those balls because he said, "If you hit a ball into the woods, somebody finds it, they're going to think I'm the one who hit that crappy shot. If they're going to find my ball in the woods, and think that I hit a crappy shot, at least I want it to really be my shot. I don't want you to end up making me look bad." He was a decent golfer. He just didn't play enough to get good at it.

Tony never spent money on anything or wanted anything other than he bought some real nice cars, but they weren't big expenditures. Tony said to me one time, "I would be happy living in a two-bedroom apartment as long as I had a big TV and cable access. That's all I'd need." That epitomized Tony. He was a very simple guy as far as wants and needs. He loved watching sports and he knew sports. He knew football, he knew basketball. One of his dreams would be to coach basketball at San Diego State. He knew that he didn't have the background where they could hire him, but he'd talk about that.

I watched the Super Bowl with Tony every year but one since 1984. It was an annual thing. I would go to his house and we would watch the Super Bowl. Tony was the commissioner of a fantasy football league that I was in. He put it together and he spent a lot of time on it too. He'd have papers all over his dining room table.

Tony had a home in Indianapolis for ten years. Indianapolis happened because Alicia was a music producer and had been for quite some time. Their daughter, Nee-Nee was and still is a singer. Alicia had a music studio out there and they had an attorney who lived in Indianapolis. They went there for business purposes and ended up liking it. They would go out there for a couple of weeks at a time during the off-season and come back when he had workouts in San Diego, and then return to Indianapolis. They were probably the only couple in the world who grew up in California and wintered in Indianapolis. It's odd when you think about it. It's the reverse of what most people do.

> They were probably the only couple in the world who grew up in California and wintered in Indianapolis.

Tony was pretty much happy all the time. Even when things weren't going well, he was still laughing about stuff and taking things one day at a time. His happiest times were just being around the house with his family, watching sports on TV, and a big barbecue going for the afternoon. That was the ultimate for Tony.

The Padres had Tony Gwynn Day and various promotions just to get people to go to games. They had a "This is Your Life" thing on Opening Day one time back when they were in really bad shape in the early '90s. I was involved in that. Before the game they introduced at home plate his grade school teacher, his high school basketball coach, his high school baseball coach, me, as his college roommate, his family of course—his mother, his kids—and various people who had been part of his life when he was growing up. When Tony got to 2,000 hits, that was a big deal in San Diego because no other Padre had achieved that milestone. That was built up, and the Padres had ceremonies around that. Then, of course, when he reached 3,000 hits that was huge. Tony would go to events like that. I wouldn't say he hated going, but he always looked forward to when the event would be over. Being the focal point of a big event like that didn't bother him, but it wasn't something he was excited about.

His passing was just a total shock for me. For me—you know how it is with a good friend or family member, you're so used to talking to them or seeing them all the time—I still think "I need to run by and see Tony," or "I need to tell Tony about this." I still go by the house and visit with Alicia a couple times a week and just check in with her. But it's tough.

We were playing in the regionals in Tulsa, Oklahoma. Tony got bored at night and we all used to stay up late all the time. Tony would go into the room and jump on the bed. I'd look at him, surprised, and ask, "What are you doing?" He'd say, "I'm bored. I'm entertaining myself." Then he'd just start laughing. He had a great laugh.

Tony and I never got in trouble on the road. We weren't that type. We were boring. We were the guys that just sat in the room all day watching TV. We didn't get into trouble, we just did what we were supposed to do.

That tournament loss to Oral Roberts senior year was awful. Our team was so good. There was just no way we thought we could lose to anyone. There were 13 guys drafted off that team. Then we faced Mike Moore, who was the best pitcher in the country that year. We just ran into a buzz saw. We were confident we were going to win the College World Series. We had great pitching, we had great defense, and we could hit.

When he played college baseball, he had about two months of batting above .400. He was worried about getting drafted. I told him, "Dude, there's no way you're not going to get drafted."

Then he went in the third round to the Padres, which was a steal. To this day Jack McKeon still laughs about that.

Tony had the same lack of confidence when he came to the baseball Hall of Fame. I'd tell him that he was going to be a first ballot selection and he wouldn't believe me. Old people are basically self-deprecating and he wasn't. He was serious. He really didn't know whether he was a first ballot Hall of Famer. I told him he was going to get 95 or 96% of the vote, so "don't even sit by the phone." He said, "I'll do good if I get 76%." I said, "You do realize what you've done in your career, don't you?" He said, "Yeah, but you know people always said I couldn't do this and I couldn't do that, I stopped stealing bases, and I didn't get a lot of home runs." I said, "Really man. You've got Gold Gloves, you've got batting titles, you've got Silver Sluggers." He said, "Well, I never won an MVP." I told him that he should have won the **MVP*** in'84. That's for darn sure.

There were two guys that I met at San Diego State that you just knew the day you met them that they were going to be major league ball players. One was Buddy Black and the other was Tony Gwynn. Buddy, because of the way he carried himself and just the cockiness in his game. You just knew he was going to be good. And Tony because he was just good.

Tony and Alicia were dating when he was at San Diego State, so if you knew Tony you knew Alicia. Alicia is a very strong woman. I always thought they complemented each other very well. Tony needed somebody like Alicia because Tony was just too nice. Tony needed somebody to say "no" for him. He had a hard time saying "no," especially early on in his career. He got better as he got older. But he just wasn't a "no" person. If he could do it for you, he'd do it. He needed somebody to put the foot down.

—**Steve Sayles**, SDSU Teammate and
former Oakland A's trainer

*In 1987, Tony Gwynn hit .370 and finished eighth in the **MVP** voting. Another year, he hit .394 and finish seventh.

Chapter Two

LET'S SKEDADDLE TO SEATTLE...AND WALLA WALLA

BRIAN'S SONG
PART DEUX

JOHN KRUK

In a story seemingly out of the playbook for "Brian's Song," John Kruk and Tony Gwynn forged a lifelong relationship, starting in of all places, Walla Walla, Washington. Kruk went on to play with the Padres, the Phillies, and the White Sox in a 10 year major-league career. He is best known for his analyst work on "Baseball Tonight" on ESPN.

I actually grew up in a town called New Creek, West Virginia that had fewer than 500 people in it. I mean it was tiny and our high school drew from the whole county.

I was drafted in 1981 by the Padres and assigned to the Northwest League. I didn't know what to expect when I left West Virginia heading to Walla Walla. I had gone as far away as Baltimore or Pittsburgh to play, but I had never really left West Virginia that much. I had never been on a plane. Just flying out there scared me to death. I didn't know what to expect. I wasn't sure I could play at the professional level. I had a lot of doubt.

I finally got to Walla Walla at night. I walked into the hotel, and there's Tony. To be honest with you, I didn't really know that the Padres existed…we didn't have cable. When I was older, a senior in high school maybe, we got cable. We got to watch the Braves, but I never watched the Padres play. I didn't even know they had a team. When I got drafted a buddy of mine brought over baseball cards and showed me cards of Dave Winfield and Randy Jones and he said, "This is who drafted you." I said, "Are you kidding me? Those uniforms are ugly!"

Tony and I hit it off immediately. He was very grounded. I was naïve about a lot of things. That may be why we hit it off so well. Tony was more than willing to help me out and teach me. I remember playing every day, and that was the hardest thing. We never had a day off. I don't think I'd have ever made the big leagues if I never met him.

I didn't know how to hit. We didn't have the stuff back then that they do now with hitting instructors and hitting camps. I didn't know the terminology of "load and trigger" and all that crap. I still don't know what that means, to be honest with you.

You knew early on that he was too good to play in the Northwest League. He was just better than everyone else. You could see it every night. He'd hit three or four balls on the "screws" and you could tell that it was a lot easier for him than for anybody else on our team. He just overmatched that league.

> "This is who drafted you." I said, "Are you kidding me? Those uniforms are ugly!"

I learned by watching him. We'd talk about hitting, but it wasn't like we broke down his swing or my swing in our conversations. He was head and shoulders above anything that I had ever thought of about hitting. He had to dumb it down for me. So I just watched him. I watched him take batting practice. Every day hitting the ball the other way the first couple rounds, and then the last round was always the free swing round where wherever the ball is pitched, that's where you hit. If the ball is inside, you pull it. If it's away, you hit it the other way. That's where I learned to hit. I didn't know how to take batting practice. I had thought you just swung. I mean, I was clueless.

He definitely saw something in me even though I hit .241. I remember the next year we worked a little bit in the spring as we hit together a lot.

In Walla Walla, we rented bikes. We pedaled everywhere we

went. We cycled everywhere. I had never played a video game in my life. There wasn't a lot going on there. With what little money we had we would pedal to the **ARCADE***. If a player hit a home run, a deli in town would make a six-foot long sandwich and the players would come and eat off that. We'd go to the arcade, then go eat, then we'd go to the ballpark every day. That's what we did, and after the game we'd ride our bikes home.

It was the best time. I mean, I couldn't believe it. I just thought that's how it worked, I didn't know any better. Obviously, Tony didn't know any better either, because, first of all, we couldn't afford to rent a car for the summer. It was bikes.

One night we arrived home and these punks pulled up in cars and started yelling some racial things at Tony. They were throwing M80 firecrackers at us. I tried to get after them. They drove off. I tried to pedal faster to catch up to their car, which was not going to happen. Tony and I had a talk that night. I said, "That's ridiculous. I'd like to find those guys. Those little punks, riding along yelling racial slurs out of a car at people on bikes."

Tony said, "Hey, it's part of life. Put it under your belt. Forget about it. We've got more important things to do. And that's getting to the big leagues." The basic message Tony was giving me was, "Don't let any distractions get in the way of getting where you want to go."

He was just more mature than most people would be at that age. I was 20 and Tony was the same or maybe 21. But I had the maturity of a teenager, an early teenager. My first reaction was to lash out, and go get them whereas Tony was, "Don't get into any trouble. Don't let anything stop you from where you want to go." I'll never forget that message that he taught me that night.

---

*When Tony was at Amarillo in the Texas League he played hundreds of games of Asteroids and **PAC-MAN**. He played them for hours on end, thinking they would help his hand-eye coordination at the plate.

In Walla Walla, Tony and I were almost inseparable. Greg Booker, later a big league pitcher and scout, was there. Greg was with us a lot. Tony and I clicked so good it was like we had known each other forever, like we grew up together. It was wonderful, a kid from West Virginia and a kid from Long Beach being so close. And trust me it was all him, 'cause I was so quiet back then, almost painfully shy. The thought of getting to know people...you know how it is, you grow up in a small town, you know everyone. Everywhere you go, you know someone. Tony recognized that. After I got comfortable, he wanted me to shut up some. Before I was so quiet.

You gotta remember I grew up in West Virginia. We started dipping at a young age there. In Walla Walla, we used to play cards. Tony had this big hankering for Coca-Cola. He would tell me, "I'll bring the drinks, you bring the snacks." So I would bring six or seven bags of potato chips and Tony would bring these big 16-ounce bottles of coke. Yeah, he loved drinking those things. That's what we did, we ate chips, drank Coke and dipped.

Did I think I was gonna make it in the big leagues? No, I quit that winter. I went home. I went back to West Virginia. I said if that's rookie ball or whatever it's called, and the players get better as they go up, I said I'm done. My dad said, "Come to work with me then. You gotta get a job. You can't be sitting around doing nothing." So I went to the factory where he worked. I worked there for half a day, and I said, "You know, this baseball thing might be worth it."

I was happy for Tony when he went to Amarillo. Nowadays the minor league kids are very aware of what their counterparts are doing within the organization. I didn't know anything about that. I was genuinely happy 'cause Tony belonged to be in a different league. He didn't deserve to stay in Walla Walla.

I was with him in Eugene, Oregon when he went into a sporting goods store at the mall and bought two bats. Our owner, if you broke a bat, you had to bring it in, and she'd give you a new one. If you were on a road trip, you bring two bats and if you break one, you gotta do something.

At the time he was using a 34-inch, 32-ounce bat when we first started. Then he found those little ones, I think they were 33 inches and 32 ounces. He started using the shorter bats. He came back on the bus and was tickled to death. He said, "Hey, look what I got. I'll be able to handle the bat easier so I can move the ball around the field better." He led off five games in a row with home runs, using those bats—a league record.

He also had me arrested up there in Eugene. I heard a knock on the door one morning. I opened up the door and it was a cop. I said, "Can I help you?" He said, "Are you John Kruk?" I said, "Yeah." And he said, "You're under arrest."

> ...lesson learned from Tony: keep your mouth shut, do it the right way, and eventually things will turn out your way.

I'm like, "Holy crap, what did I do?" He put me in the car, the whole deal. Then, I look over and I see Tony laughing his head off. I said, "What are you laughing at?" And he came out and told me that the man was the dad of his college roommate and was a real cop. His old roomie came up to see Tony, and Tony thought he'd have some fun and have his buddy's dad arrest me.

I went to my first MLB spring training in 1986. It was obvious that Tony, Kevin McReynolds, and Carmelo Martinez were the three starters, and Bobby Brown was the fourth outfielder. I looked at it that I had to be really good to stick. We went to San Diego first to have our physicals. We had our physicals in the morning and afterwards we got in our cars and drove to Yuma. We got there mid-afternoon, and Tony walked right over and said, "Let's go hit." I was like, "What?" He said, "Let's go hit." So we went and hit that day.

The writing was on the wall for me. I wasn't go going to go back to AAA for a third year. I was going to see if they would either trade me or release me if I didn't make the team. That was what was on my mind. But as things played out, I had a great spring. I led in every offensive category in spring training. Then we went to Las Vegas to play some exhibition games. That's where the AAA team was. They called me in after the second game and told me that I was staying there. Steve Boros was then the manager. They told me if someone got hurt I'd be the first one they'd call. I told them, "I'm going home. You can release me or trade me or something, but I'm not playing here another year."

Tony didn't give me many talks. He gave me a few, and that's one where he said, "Go do what they say. You know how it is, 162 games in the season, but if you pout and mope and you get off to a bad start, you're done. Your baseball career is over."

I said, "Screw that. I'm done. I ain't doing this." I was getting ready to drive home. Then Bobby Brown retired. He came over and said, "Congratulations, you made the team." I said, "What are you talking about? Boros just called me in and told me I'm staying here." Bobby Brown said, "I just went in and told them I'm retired. You deserve to play."

Now I'm like, "Oh my God. I have to apologize to everyone who I'd cursed at." So lesson learned from Tony: keep your mouth shut, do it the right way, and eventually things will turn out your way.

It was amazing. After I started playing more in the big leagues, like my fifth, sixth, seventh year, Tony's wisdom and advice really registered with me. Not that we're owned by the team, but they're paying you, they can make or break you. If you lash out and rebel like I did, they might not want you. Tony got that early. I didn't realize it till later in my career that the things he was telling me were the things I should pay attention to.

The year after Walla Walla, I was really excited to hear that he got called up to the big leagues. He was the first guy that I had ever known that made it to the big leagues. It was really neat that here was a guy I was close to, he's in the big leagues, and he's tearing it up. In Yuma, when you go to spring training, you share basically the same building, but there's a wall in between the big league clubhouse and the minor league clubhouse. The equipment manager would come to the minor league side and say, "Hey, Tony wants to talk to you." We would talk. They had one of those doors where the top opened and the bottom opened too. The bottom usually stayed closed. They'd open up the top and Tony and I would talk. He'd give me a glove or a bat. Terry Kennedy and I used the same size bat, so Tony would get me one of Terry's bats to use. Some of the guys in the minor league complex were jealous of the fact that here I am getting a glove every year and big league bats from Tony. We were on our own for all that stuff then. It wasn't like now where everyone has a glove and bat contract. It made me feel special. It made me feel like if Tony didn't think I could make it, he wouldn't waste his time getting me stuff.

Back in Walla Walla that first year, I never dreamed I'd make it in the big leagues or that one day I'd be a TV analyst. But you knew Tony was going to hit, and you knew he was going to win batting titles, and maybe even that he'd be in the Hall of Fame. When you saw him play, you knew you'd better get to know him quick because he was going to be away from you soon.

Tony and I didn't get to speak much in the winter during the off-seasons, but when we got together again for spring training it was like I had just seen him the day before. He was the one I looked forward to seeing, because I knew he was going to be a big help to me. The way he could break down pitchers, and all that stuff. When I made the team he was genuinely happy for me. He felt that I could help the team win.

As I got older, I had an ability to make Tony laugh, no matter what. If you ever heard his laugh... I would try to entertain him, but really it was for my entertainment just to hear him laugh, 'cause it was special. He was doing some college stuff for ESPN when I first got to Bristol. He was up in Connecticut so again we would hang out and talk.

Tony became a contact hitter in the big leagues. He thought that he would help the team better if he got on base more, rather than trying to hit a home run every time. But he was always an aggressive base runner, a smart runner. He rarely made a base running mistake. He won his five Gold Gloves through work. Work, work, work.

> ...it was for my entertainment just to hear him laugh, 'cause it was special.

At the plate, Tony called it the "steer the ship." You know, with the big wheel. The right arm goes down, the left arm goes up. I didn't have any proper training, I would just wing it. Since I played left field, he'd play right. He taught me how to do the 360-degree turn on balls down the left field line. I never did that before, I just caught it and turned or whatever. He basically taught me how to throw.

My son is 12 years old. He knows me as a Phillie, because he was born when we lived just outside of Philadelphia, before we moved to Florida. So, he's a Phillies fan. When I work with him and his Little League teammates on hitting, it's all stuff that Tony taught me. My son got into wanting to learn more about Tony Gwynn. He'd say, "Tell me more about Tony Gwynn." Pretty much every coach my son's had, that's who they want to talk to me about. Not Ozzie Smith or Lenny Dykstra or Darren Daulton, they'd go, "How good was Gwynn? How good was Gwynn? Was he as good as what we thought he was?"

He was better! I'd tell them that "All you guys see are the batting titles he won. You should see the work he put in. He was a workaholic." Tony got me early in my career. He said, "We're going to go hit. Every day on the road we're going to go hit early." And when we were at home, we'd go early. One day when we were at home, I said, "Hey Tony why do you go early every day to hit?" He said, "You see where the light is? When you go to regular batting practice, there are shadows. I don't like hitting in those shadows." I'm like, "Who'd have thought of that?"

I became aware of Tony's health problems like everyone else when it became public. I kept in touch with his agent. In later years I tried to communicate with Tony forever with no success. I tried to call him and would leave messages, but he would never call back. I saw Chris at the winter meetings a few years ago and said, "Hey, is your brother ever going to get back to me?" He said, "John, he's got all your messages. He appreciates them, but he just doesn't want to talk to anyone right now."

I was still with the Padres when I quit dipping. It gave me real bad heartburn. Subsequently, I've had my esophagus wrapped because of the bad heartburn I was having. I had to go in and have doctors wrap my esophagus because it was burning.

Tony never wanted to talk about himself. It seemed to me that he didn't want to burden his friends with what was ailing him. I'm sure you know people, they get a hangnail, they'll call you and say, "I've got the worst hangnail ever." Tony didn't want to bother people with any of his issues.

His agent, John Boggs told me that he seemed to be getting worse about a month before his death. I was doing an Angels-Braves game in Atlanta. We had a manager's meeting with Mike Scioscia, who had just got back from **BOB WELCH'S*** funeral in Arizona. I guess Dave Stewart was there and some others. Scioscia said, "Hey man, what have you heard from Tony?" I said, "The last I heard he was doing okay." He said, "I heard different. I heard he could go at any time."

I said, "What?" I was out in the field, I was in a fog and I'm thinking, "There's no way. There's no way this can happen." So I talked with Terry Pendleton, who was coaching the Braves, and I told him about it. He said, "Oh man, I didn't hear that." I said, "I can't believe it. This could happen any time."

*The only time Tony Gwynn ever struck out three times in a game was against **BOB WELCH**, who died one week before Tony.

The next day I had an early flight from Atlanta to Florida and when I got there I had five or six text messages: "I can't believe what happened to Tony." "Can't believe this." "Can't believe it." So I called Chris Gwynn. It went to the answering machine and I left a message, "Hey Chris, please tell me this isn't true what I'm hearing." Chris called me that night and said Tony was going fast. Since then, I talked to John Boggs, and he confirmed that Tony had passed away. Chris called me that night, very upset. We talked for a while. I was just in shock. To this day, I still can't believe it. I don't want to believe it.

Without Tony Gwynn, I don't get to play in the big leagues. He had the biggest influence on my career. In the big leagues, Tony was the one who kept pushing. Push, push, push. Let's go hit. Let's go hit. Let's go work. Let's make ourselves better.

I remember one year I was leading him in hitting. It was July. We were in **MONTRÉAL***, before going to Baltimore. I said, "I'm taking the batting title away from you this year." He said, "What?" I said, "I'm going to win the batting title. You're going to have to present me with the Silver Slugger Award next year at Jack Murphy on Opening Day. I'm takin' this thing." He looked at me and he goes, "We'll see!" Then, in that Montréal series, he went 8 for 10. I never caught up.

We didn't have to communicate with each other to know that when we saw each other it was just like old times. He would just sit there and listen to me tell stories, and he'd laugh. When I got traded to the Phillies and would come to San Diego to play, Tony would never come in the visitor's clubhouse to say "Hi." But, he'd send his son Anthony into the clubhouse every

*Gwynn's most frustrating at bat occurred in **MONTRÉAL** in 1986 in a game that the Padres lost 10-1. The Expos ran out of pitchers, and brought in infielder Vance Law from second base to pitch to Gwynn. Gwynn grounded out. He later said, "You probably never heard of Vance Law. But I carry that at-bat around in my mind every day."

time. Tony would send him in to chat with me. And Tony Jr. would say, "My dad said he'll see you out there on the field."

I was there in San Diego for Tony's private memorial service. Chris Gwynn called me and asked if I would come and speak. Then Alicia sent me an email asking if I could come out to San Diego and speak. She said that I was a big part of Tony's life. She told me that she had heard so many stories about some of the crazy things we did. She said, "Tony got a kick out of you." I'd have tried to go anyway, even if I wasn't invited. It was a private family ceremony, and the family asked me to speak.

It was probably the hardest thing I've ever had to do in my life. I was still in shock. I didn't know what to say. John Boggs and some others told me to just talk about what he meant to you. How do you say that? How do you talk about someone who meant that much to you? It just came out. Whatever I said just came out at that moment. It was the hardest thing I've ever had to do in my life.

Then, a few days later, we reminisced about Tony on *Baseball Tonight*. We talked about what he meant to me, what he meant to San Diego, and what he meant to baseball. That was easy.

Without question, Tony's passing will leave a void in the rest of my life. As long as I'm covering baseball, Tony's going to be a part of that. Every time I see a guy making mistakes, hitting or running, I think about what I learned from Tony. So, his name is going to keep coming up. When he's the best player you ever played with, and you saw how hard he worked, it's not hard to have him incorporated in a discussion.

I get asked why I think he turned down millions of dollars to stay in San Diego. It's because he was happy and his family was happy there. I told him one time that he could get so much more money from the Yankees. He looked at me and he goes, "But then I'd have to tell Alicia and the kids that we're moving to New York." I said, "Yeah, that's probably not good, is it?" He was just happy in San Diego. That was his life. It wasn't about playing twenty years, or getting 3,000 hits with the Padres. It was nothing about that. That was going to happen. It's just that's where he was happy. It's not like he lived an elaborate life. "This is where I want to be. This is where my family is happy. This is where I'm happy and we're not moving."

He used to talk about what it was like to play for San Diego State, so I wasn't surprised when he became the baseball coach there. I actually had a long discussion with him, because I would like to coach college softball. He said, "Oh man. It can be a headache. You stop on the way for dinner, and you have to count every penny. If you overspend your budget or whatever, the NCAA will come down on you. It's more work than it's anything." He said, "The coaching is the great part." Tony was the kind of person who wouldn't let someone else watch the budget and all that stuff. I'll tell you this though, can you imagine him coming to someone's house and saying, "I want your son to come and play for me at San Diego State." How do you say "No?"

Of all the people I played with and became friends with and teammates with, he was the most influential. One year, I finally got a three-year deal with the Phillies. At the time it was pretty good money, almost seven and a half million dollars for three years. Here's the great thing about Tony: Normally when we played the Padres in Philadelphia, they had just come from New York or Montréal or some National League East team. Of course, he got on base a couple times a night. At first base, he would always tell me something helpful like, "The Mets just called up this new pitcher. Here's how he'll try to get you out. This guy did this. This guy did that." So, I had a great game plan when we played that team.

I remember one time, we looked at each other and he said, "Can you believe they're paying two guys that met in 1981 in Walla Walla, Washington... Who'd ever have thought that we'd get paid millions of dollars to play a game?" We both just started laughing. It was unbelievable.

I miss him every day. I think about him every day.

THERE'S A SING SING IN WALLA WALLA, NORTH-NORTHWEST OF TOWN

JIM BUCHAN

Jim Buchan retired as Sports Editor at the Walla Walla Union-Bulletin Newspaper *in 2014 after a long and distinguished career. His golf handicap gets lower every day.*

Ask any Walla Wallan what his or her hometown is best known for and the patented answer will be the sweetest onions and the boldest wines you can possibly imagine. No one mentions the Washington State Penitentiary on the north side of town.

And then they always add: "Oh, and did you know that Tony Gwynn began his professional baseball career right here in Walla Walla?"

Everyone in Walla Walla is proud of it. And with good reason.

I don't know that any of us realized what we were witnessing when Gwynn stepped into the batter's box at Borleske Stadium for the first time. I certainly know I didn't on the few occasions I watched Gwynn play, and my friend Gene Adams concurred.

Adams, whose full time job back then was director of financial aid services at Whitman College, spent his summers in those days as the Walla Walla Padres public address announcer and also the team's official scorekeeper.

I asked him the other day if he had any indication of Gwynn's potential. He said, "No. But I was not a talent scout, either.

"Clearly he was very good, but I couldn't imagine the Hall of Fame and all of those batting championships. But he was much more talented than any of the other rookies."

To give you an idea, he only played 42 games for Walla Walla that summer, but he hit .406, and extrapolated over a full Major League season, it would have been .406 with 40 home runs, 140 RBIs, and 60 stolen bases. To give you another idea of how good that was, John Kruk, his teammate that season and a life-time .300 hitter in the Major Leagues, hit .241.

After the 42 games, Tony was promoted to Reno. But because, 1981, that summer, was the year of the air traffic controller's strike and then firings, he couldn't get to Reno, so they sent him to Amarillo instead, in the AA Texas League. All he did in Amarillo was hit.462.

Gene and I remembered a conversation we had with Gwynn in the Padres dugout that summer. He was 21 years old at the time, just graduated from San Diego State and quite mature. We were observing the other players in batting practice—18-and 19-year-olds acting like immature teens, which they were— and Tony was not amused.

"He said, 'They have to grow up sometime,' or something to that effect. 'They need to be more serious.' He took the game seriously even at that stage of his career.

Gene said his lasting overall impression is that Gwynn was a terrific guy. He said that he was more impressed with him as a person than he was as a player, and he was a very good player.

Gwynn did not have a car in Walla Walla that summer—most of the players didn't—so he, John Kruk, and Greg Booker used to ride bicycles everywhere. It was on a road trip to Eugene, Oregon where Tony walked into a sporting goods store and bought a 32 ounce, 32½-inch Louisville Slugger, and that's the type of bat he used for the majority of his career.

In those days, Walla Walla was the Class A team for the Padres in the Northwest League. Now we don't have professional baseball anymore, but we do have the Walla Walla Sweets of the West Coast League, which is a college summer league that uses wooden bats. But the Northwest League and the Walla Walla Padres were once a big deal in this town.

Walla Walla has a rich history of professional baseball, particularly with the Padres. The Phillies brought professional ball to Borleske Stadium in 1969 and remained for three seasons. When they left town, the Hawaiian Islanders of the Pacific Coast League stocked the team with players for one season. It's very unusual that a Triple-A team would have a farm team of its own. The Padres came in 1973 and they sent many of their top prospects here. Ozzie Smith was here four years before Tony got here.

One of the more popular players was a handsome young man named Kurt Russell. Russell was a good player and he hit .325 in his time in Walla Walla. He was 21 years old, but his season was cut short due to the filming and July release of the movie *Now You See It, Now You Don't*, one of several Walt Disney movies that he starred in during his early years as an actor. Of course, he went on to make movies like *Backdraft* and *Tombstone*, and has been a partner with Goldie Hawn for many years.

A lot of other Padres got their start here. Padres like Andy Hawkins, Eric Show, Dane Iorg, Tucker Ashford, and Broderick Perkins. Walla Walla is also the birthplace of a couple of Major League managers. The former Oakland A's manager Bob Geren and former Milwaukee Brewers and Chicago Cubs manager Tom Trebelhorn got their start here. Every night on national television we can watch our former players John Kruk and Mitch Williams do analyst jobs.

But, like I said, sweet onions, Tony Gwynn, and fine wine are still points of pride in the Walla Walla Valley.

IRONICALLY ENOUGH, IT WAS RAINING THE LAST TIME I WAS IN SEATTLE

PETE BROWN

Pete Brown, 72, is a lifelong sports nut who is retired and lives in Seattle with his wife. He graduated from Dartmouth College and has had stints at playing, coaching and officiating a variety of sports, as well as being a high-school math teacher, college dean of admissions and selling sports cards and memorabilia.

My first glimpse of Tony Gwynn came in June 1981, the season-opener of the Walla Walla Padres Northwest League baseball team. Even in that first game, I realized that the Padres had something special in Gwynn, who had been assigned to Walla Walla after being drafted in the **THIRD ROUND*** out of San Diego State.

In his first game as a pro, on opening night in Walla Walla, WA, against the Salem Senators, an Angels farm team, Gwynn went 3 for 5, with a triple, a walk, two stolen bases, two runs scored, and a strikeout. He started in centerfield, walked in his first at-bat, stole second on the first pitch, and third on the

---

*In the 1981 draft, Tony Gwynn was the fourth player drafted by the Padres, even though he went in the **THIRD ROUND**. Kevin McReynolds, a University of Arkansas outfielder, went with the sixth overall pick in the first round. A catcher from the University of Miami went 26th in the first round, and Miami of Ohio right-handed pitcher, Bill Long, went in the second round. Gwynn was not even the first player drafted from that San Diego State team. Bobby Meacham was the eighth overall pick in the first-round by the Yankees.

next pitch, before scoring a pitch later on a bad pickoff throw to third base. On his second time at bat he got his first professional hit, a single off a pitcher named Buck Long.

As it turned out, I only had about seven weeks to watch him play. After 43 games with the Rookie League, Class A, short-season team, he was called up to Amarillo in the Class AA Texas League. What a seven weeks it was. By the time he left, Gwynn led the Northwest League in nearly every offensive category, including batting average (.331), stolen bases (17), and home runs (12). Even though he played only part of that season for Walla Walla, he was voted the league MVP at the end of the season. Gwynn's salary at Walla Walla was $500 per month.

I attended many games that season and still have an official 1981 Walla Walla Padres program (price 50 cents) autographed by Tony. I made a note that the game of the program (on July 5, 1981) was won by the Padres 5-4 on a three-run walk-off home run by Tony Gwynn in the bottom of the ninth inning. I recognize many of the names on my scorecard from that game, played against the Bellingham Mariners, including Phil Bradley and Rickey Nelson, who later played with the Seattle Mariners. Not on my scorecard but also on the Bellingham roster that year was Mark Langston. On the Padres side of the scorecard, I recognize Gwynn, John Kruk and Greg Booker as future major-leaguers Gwynn is listed at 5 feet 11, and 185 pounds, and John Kruk at 5-10 and 175.

... "And I'm the reason that Tony Gwynn is now an outfielder!"

At the end of the 1981 season, the Walla Walla Padres held what they called a "bat scramble". All the cracked bats from the season were put in a big pile near second base, and kids in the stadium were allowed to line up along the first-base line. When the whistle blew, the kids ran toward the pile of bats and could grab as many as they could carry back to the stands. My 12-year-old and 10-year-old sons each came away with three or four cracked bats inscribed with "Genuine Walla Walla Padres Louisville Slugger".

Most of the bats have long since been taped up, used for batting practice, re-broken and discarded. The exception was one of the bats my 10-year-old won. He said that he had already secured three bats and was in a final tug of war with "a great big kid" over a final bat when he looked down at the knob of the bat and saw that it was inscribed in magic marker with "T. Gwynn". He gave one more "tremendous tug", and the bat came loose. He hauled his prized possession back to the stands.

In 1988, while I was living in Portland, I had lunch in Seattle with a business acquaintance named John. The conversation turned to baseball, as it often did with me, and I mentioned that Tony Gwynn was my favorite player.

"I played on the same Little League team with Tony Gwynn growing up in Long Beach," John said. "And I'm the reason that Tony Gwynn is now an outfielder!"

I asked John to explain, and he said he had been a 10-year-old veteran on the team when Tony joined the team at age 9. The coach had asked Tony what position he would like to play, as he did with all new players. The new kid responded that he was left-handed and played first base. The coach explained that John also was left-handed and had played first base the previous year.

"Tony, why don't you go out and try center field?" the coach said.

In 1990 while I still lived in Portland, Tony Gwynn was the "autograph guest" at a local card show. I took the "T. Gwynn" Walla Walla Padres bat and a 1983 Topps Gwynn Rookie Card to the card show and purchased autograph tickets. Tony stopped everything when he came to sign the bat, talking for at least 10 minutes after hoisting the bat and looking it over.

"This is the real thing, and it's so much bigger than the little toothpick of a bat I use in the major leagues to increase my bat speed and give me better bat control," he said. "The Walla Walla folks never asked us what size bat we wanted. They just said, 'Here is your bat—hit.'"

Tony was such an engaging, outgoing guy that it further cemented him as my favorite player.

Fast forward to Seattle in 2001 when the All-Star Game was played at Safeco Field. I was living in Seattle and had been lucky enough to win two tickets to all of the All-Star Game events including the player banquet the night before the game. Ichiro had arrived in Seattle and wound up winning the American League Rookie of the Year and MVP awards with the Mariners. At the All-Star break, he was the leading vote getter for a starting spot in the American League outfield. **CAL RIPKEN JR.*** and Tony Gwynn, both in their final seasons, were honored before the game for their outstanding careers.

At the large buffet dinner the night before the All-Star Game, I kept my eye out for both Ichiro and Tony Gwynn, since attendees could hobnob with the players during the outdoor meal held at a restaurant along the pier. Ichiro needed a police escort to get him past the crowds who were hanging around the entrance to the restaurant, and he ended up eating inside in a private room, so I never had a chance to meet him. I spotted Tony, though, and introduced myself, congratulated him on a great career, and told him that I had seen him play in Walla Walla.

Tony asked me where I was living now, and I replied Seattle.

"I'll bet everyone in Seattle is having a great time watching Ichiro hit," he said. "He is a fantastic talent and has a unique approach!"

I'll never forget watching Tony Gwynn play in his first professional games, and those encounters with him years later. What a positive person, a classy human being and a great ambassador for the game of baseball.

---

*When Lou Piniella played minor league baseball in Aberdeen, SD, the team's batboy was **CAL RIPKEN JR.** Ripken's dad managed the team. Ironically, the Ripkens lived in Aberdeen, Maryland in the off-season.

Chapter Three

A TONY GWYNN ANTHOLOGY

A Compendium Reader for Tony Gwynn Readers

A SHORT STORY
FROM A LONG MEMORY

BILL PLASCHKE

Los Angeles Times *writer*

It was 27 years ago this summer, one of my first days of work at the *Los Angeles Times*, and I was hopelessly lost.

Walking into the San Diego Padres clubhouse to introduce myself as the new beat guy for the *Times'* San Diego County edition, I was stopped by a wave of angry noise.

Larry Bowa, the manager, was howling in his office. Goose Gossage, the veteran reliever, was grumbling in front of his locker. Garry Templeton, the longtime shortstop, was waving his arms in front of another locker.

The air was filled with hostility. The scene was the kind of madness that can only happen on an aging and ill-equipped baseball team owned by the wife of the man who built the McDonald's empire, Joan Kroc. The Padres were headed toward 97 losses and I was headed back out the clubhouse door to catch my breath when I heard a cackling laugh that I still can hear today.

"Hey, new guy, come back in here," shouted Tony Gwynn. "It's crazy, but you'll get used to it."

I returned, and headed straight for Gwynn's locker, where I spent much of the next two seasons witnessing a unique combination of greatness and grace, toughness and kindness, heavenly skills and earthly touch.

Tony Gwynn died at age 54, and the loss to the humanity of the sports world is incalculable.

He was one of the greatest pure swingers ever, a Hall of Famer with 3,141 hits. But more important, in a sports world filled with arrogance and vitriol, he was unmatched as a human being. That locker that served as my refuge was everyone's refuge, the neighborhood grocery, all welcome, all treated as an equal.

Even during the two occasions when his Padres reached the World Series, he acted as if he was still at Long Beach Poly High, just a lucky kid hanging out with friends.

He was always smiling through the sweat of his seemingly constant work. He was always willing to answer any question about anything: hitting, the Lakers, life, and always with a wisdom that didn't demean, but empowered.

"OK, listen, I'll tell you how it works..." he would say, and then explain everything from an opposite-field swing to the best way to handle a tempestuous teammate.

On days when it seemed the entire Padres team was angrily staring at me for something negative I'd written, Gwynn would be the first to shout my name and bellow out one of those brilliant laughs and call me over to settle my nerves.

"You're not mad, too?" I would ask him.

"Oh, no, I'm also mad at you," he would say. "But as long you're over here talking to me, none of those crazy guys will rip our head off."

For an entire generation of sportswriters, Tony Gwynn was a teacher, a touchstone, a friend. For me, during one frightening time in 1988, he was also a baby sitter.

The Padres were playing in **CINCINNATI***. I had brought my

*In April of 1957, Don Hoak of the **REDS** was on second base and Gus Bell was on first when Wally Post hit a double-play ground ball. Hoak fielded the ball with his bare hands and tossed the ball to Johnny Logan, the Milwaukee Braves shortstop. Hoak was automatically out for interference—but not the batter—and the Reds thereby avoided an easy double-play. The Reds did the same subterfuge three times that year before the rule was changed.

15-year-old brother on the trip. When I returned to my hotel room after a Saturday afternoon game, Andrew was missing. I called the front desk. I called his mom. In a panic, I ran down to the lobby, where I discovered my brother eating pizza and talking hitting with Tony Gwynn.

It was not surprising that Gwynn turned down millions of dollars to spend his entire 20-year career in San Diego, where he became the smiling face of an often-forlorn organization. He didn't care about the money. He cared about the community. He cared about his friends.

In his later years when our paths crossed, as he became a television commentator and then the head coach at San Diego State, Gwynn would always greet me with a hug and a few memories about the crazy old days. Moments after we parted, I would turn around and see him hugging someone else.

He was perhaps baseball's finest ambassador, even to the point of using his own illness as a warning to current players, as he insisted that his cancer of the salivary gland was caused by his constant use of chewing tobacco.

Three years ago, one of Tony Gwynn's greatest legacies showed up at Chavez Ravine. It was his son, Tony Gwynn Jr., who spent two modest seasons as a Dodgers outfielder. When I approached Tony Jr. for our first interview, I felt so old — until he gave me that Gwynn hug and that Gwynn laugh.

Tony Jr. never flinched at the burden of a baseball player carrying the Gwynn name. He acted lucky to be there, and glad to have others along for the ride. His father would have been proud.

"I know this sounds funny, but I gotta tell you, I love your dad," I told him once.

"That's not funny at all," he said. "Because I do, too."

In the end, truly, Tony Gwynn's greatest achievement was not that he was so admired or emulated, but that he was so loved.

QUICK HITS & INTERESTING BITS

My most memorable encounter with Mr. Padre came in August 1995, when I was assigned to write a profile of him for the *Denver Post's* Baseball Monday section. Before newspapers put the squeeze on writers and insisted that everything be presented in bite-size chunks, we had the luxury of spending lots of time with subjects and going well beyond the surface insights that are captured in tweets.

I remember arriving mid-afternoon for a 7 p.m. game and getting a stiff-arm from a security guard, who told me I was too early and would not be allowed to enter the home clubhouse at Jack Murphy Stadium. As I prepared for a lengthy wait, Gwynn suddenly emerged from the clubhouse, beckoned me with his index finger and invited me into his lair in the video room.

I might as well been privy to a conversation with Stephen Hawking on gravitational singularity theorems. Gwynn had personally invested almost $100,000 in video monitors, an edit board, and assorted other gizmos that he gradually shared with his fellow San Diego hitters. For more than an hour, he sat in a chair wearing a backward baseball cap and conducted a tutorial that helped explain how he earned the dual nickname of "Captain Video."

Gwynn walked me through his thought process on assorted plate appearances and laid out the specifics of his batting practice regimen. He began each batting practice session by laying out a cursory drag bunt, then began spraying line drives all over the field with a routine that he called "carving." In my story for the *Post*, I described him peppering the Jack Murphy outfield with "cowhide rainbows."

All those batting titles and those 3,141 career hits produced relatively modest earnings for Gwynn, who maxed out with a $6.3 million salary in 2000. He took some grief from the players' association for giving the Padres so many hometown discounts. But he shrugged off the critiques, and kept re-signing, because his heart was in San Diego and he understood the synergy that can exist between Joe Fan and the face of the franchise. It meant something to him that the same people who had watched him play point guard for the San Diego State Aztecs were able to celebrate all those Padres' milestones firsthand.

The Gwynn family name lives on in Major League Baseball. Chris Gwynn, a true pro who carried the mantle of "Tony's brother" with grace and goodwill for so many years, is now the Seattle Mariners' farm director, and Tony Gwynn Jr, is in his eighth big league season. Young Tony doesn't have his father's ability to hit, but he is relentlessly upbeat, nice to everyone who crosses his path, and respectful of the game and the people in it. He embodies the positive attitudes that his parents valued, and can rest assured that he made Tony Sr. proud

—**Jerry Crasnick**, formerly with the
Denver Post, now with ESPN.COM

Also joining our team during my debut 1982 season was this little fat guy from a local college who Jack McKeon had insisted on drafting in the third round the previous year, even though most scouts thought his bat was slow and he'd never be able to field. Eight batting titles and four Gold Gloves later, maybe you've heard of the guy. Name of Gwynn.

McKeon's promotion of Tony to the big leagues in my first year proved to be the nicest thing anybody has ever done for me. I don't think I've ever had a player who worked harder and cared more and was more deserving of his rewards.

Particularly in the field, where Tony was originally a hack. He knew he had to work on being a decent fielder, so he worked until he became a great one. And don't think his batting titles came naturally either. With that big butt and funny walk, nothing for him was ever easy.

Take Gwynn's first season, on an August night in Pittsburgh. He wasn't playing, so he was down at the end of the bench talking to pitcher Eric Show. With Show being a high thinker (translated: strange agent), it was only natural that instead of baseball, they were talking about politics. Show was quizzing Gwynn on what he called *Twenty Things Every*

American Should Know—questions about Congress and stuff like that. Poor Tony couldn't figure out any of the answers. Most people couldn't, which was Show's point. But to make things worse, when they reach the 20th question, I shouted for Tony to enter the game as a defensive replacement. He ran to the field with, as he later explained, his mind still spinning. He dove for the first fly ball hit to him and broke his wrist. So much for quiz shows that didn't involve the manager.

Even the public acclaim that Tony rightly deserved didn't come easy for him. This always bothered me because I was so fond of him. His peers knew he just might be baseball's best player, but the San Diego fans always seem to cheer louder for a guy like infielder **TIM FLANNERY**,* who'd broken in with the Padres three years before Gwynn. The reasons for this iniquity are as simple as they are stupid. Flannery is the ideal southern Californian. He surfs. His hair is blond. And of course, he is white. The players used to call Flannery and his wife, Donna, "Ken and Barbie." The way the San Diego fans reacted to them, you'd have thought they were Charles and Di. They gave Flannery standing ovations on opening day, with every hit, with every dive at third base. They'd cheer so much you'd wondered if you were watching Babe Ruth with a tan.

You were not. This is not to say Flannery isn't a great guy. He's the best. But he never was a great player, as he knows himself. And he's certainly not the kind of player around which a pennant winner is built. Above all, he's not even in the same category as Gwynn, who it seems got cheered only when he reached a batting milestone or threw a guy out at home plate from the right field corner. Flannery wouldn't recognize the sound of a boo; Gwynn couldn't forget it. In any controversy Gwynn was always the bad guy, the one taking abuse from the right field bleachers. My only gripe with the otherwise

*__**TIM FLANNERY**__, in addition to playing 11 years in the big leagues, performed with Willie Nelson, Jackson Browne, and Jimmy Buffet. Flannery was a singer, songwriter, and guitarist.

wonderful San Diego fans is that they will never let Tony Gwynn forget that he doesn't look like Tim Flannery.

—Manager **Dick Williams** in his book *No More Mr. Nice Guy*

I still remember everything. Doug Rader was our Triple-A manager and I had made a baserunning mistake that cost us the game that night. I thought for sure I was being called into his office so he could chew me out for that. He went through the whole thing, ripped my butt, then said, "Anyway, you're going to join the Padres tomorrow." And after that sank in, he said, "And by the way, Steve Carlton will be pitching."

Well, for six hours, I'm sitting around in Honolulu worrying to death about that, but when my plane got in, I found out it wasn't going to be Carlton after all. But Mike Krukow. Now, nothing against Krukie, but that was a big relief.

First at-bat, sac fly... I ended up 2-for-4. I made it, and on my first hit, **PETE ROSE*** trailed the play, shook my hand, and said, "Don't catch me all in one day, kid." Wow. My folks were there, my whole family, they saw it all.

After the game all my buddies from San Diego State were there.... It was a pass list of a couple of dozen. To debut for your hometown team in your own hometown against a team with Rose on it, (Mike) Schmidt, Gary Matthews, Steve Carlton— you never forget that.

—**Josh Lewin** quoting Tony Gwynn in *You Never Forget Your First*

*On the same day Tony Gwynn made his major league debut, Luke Appling homered into the stands in the inaugural Old Timers All-Star Game at RFK Stadium. Appling was 75 years old. After the game, Appling said, "I sure am glad the season is over!"...In Gwynn's debut game, **PETE ROSE** collected hit number 3800.

BOXSCORE

Philadelphia Phillies 7, San Diego Padres 6

Game Played on Monday, July 19, 1982 (Night) at Jack Murphy Stadium

Philadelphia	0	2	4	0	0	0	1	0	0	—	7	10	0
San Diego	2	1	0	0	0	0	0	3	0	—	6	12	1

BATTING

Philadelphia Phillies	AB	R	H	RBI	BB	K	PO	A
Dernier cf	4	1	1	0	1	0	3	0
Rose 1b	5	2	2	0	0	0	9	1
Matthews lf	5	1	1	2	0	2	2	0
Schmidt 3b	5	1	2	1	0	1	1	0
Diaz c	5	1	2	2	0	2	5	0
Robinson rf	3	0	1	1	0	1	0	0
Vukovich ph-rf	1	0	1	1	0	0	1	0
Trillo 2b	4	0	0	0	0	2	2	2
DeJesus ss	3	0	0	0	1	0	3	3
Krukow p	0	0	0	0	0	0	1	1
Monge p	2	1	0	0	1	1	0	1
Lyle p	0	0	0	0	0	0	0	0
R. Reed p	0	0	0	0	0	0	0	2
Totals	37	7	10	7	3	9	27	10

BATTING

2B: Robinson (5, off Show); Vukovich (6, off Show)
HR: Schmidt (13, 2nd inning off Curtis, 0 on, 0 out); Diaz (15, 2nd inning off Curtis, 0 on, 0 out)
SH: Monge (2, off Show)

BASERUNNING

SB: Matthews (14, 3rd base off Chiffer/Kennedy); DeJesus (14, 2nd base off Chiffer/Kennedy); Dernier (37, 2nd base off Show/Kennedy)

San Diego Padres	AB	R	H	RBI	BB	K	PO	A
Richards lf	4	1	2	0	1	0	0	0
Flannery 2b	2	1	1	1	1	0	2	1
Pittman ph-2b	1	0	0	0	0	0	0	1
Jones ph	1	0	0	0	0	0	0	0
DeLeon p	0	0	0	0	0	0	0	0
Templeton ss	5	0	1	1	0	1	1	4
Lezcano rf	4	1	2	1	0	0	1	0
Gwynn cf	4	1	2	1	0	1	5	0
Kennedy c	4	1	0	0	1	1	9	0
Perkins 1b	4	1	2	0	0	0	9	0
Salazar 3b	4	0	1	1	0	0	0	0
Curtis p	1	0	0	0	0	1	0	2
Chiffer p	0	0	0	0	0	0	0	0
Edwards ph	1	0	0	0	0	0	0	0
Show p	1	0	0	0	0	1	0	1
Bevacqua ph	1	0	1	1	0	0	0	0
Wiggins pr-2b	0	0	0	0	0	0	0	0
Totals	37	6	12	6	3	5	27	9

FIELDING

E: Flannery (8)

BATTING

2B: Lezcano (17, off Monge); Gwynn (1, off Monge)
HR: Lezcano (9, 8th inning off Monge 0 on, 0 out)
SH: Lezcano (2, off Krukow)
SF: Gwynn (1, off Krukow)

BASERUNNING

SB: Richards (20, 2nd base off Krukow/Diaz)

PITCHING

Philadelphia Phillies	IP	H	HR	R	ER	BB	K
Krukow	1.1	6	0	3	3	0	1
Monge W(4-0)	5.2	4	1	3	3	2	4
Lyle	0.2	1	0	0	0	1	0
R. Reed SV(2)	1.1	1	0	0	0	0	0
Totals	9.0	12	1	6	6	3	5

San Diego Padres	IP	H	HR	R	ER	BB	K
Curtis L(6-6)	2	5	2	6	6	1	1
Chiffer	2	1	0	0	0	1	1
Show	4	4	0	1	1	1	5
DeLeon	1	0	0	0	0	0	2
Totals	9	10	2	7	7	3	9

Umpires: Frank Pulli, Doug Harvey, Bob Davidson, Jerry Crawford
Time of Game: 2:48   Attendance: 33,558

Let me tell you one more. Now it's 1981 and Tony Gwynn was playing at Long Beach State for San Diego State. This goes back to when my boss Freddie and I were still getting used to each other.

So we were going to go over to see Mark Davis play. So we get there and Freddie says, "Which one is Mark?"

"Here he is. He's standing right next to us."

Well, I've never seen Freddie run so fast in his life. He took out his watch and ran over toward the first base line and leaned over the fence. Mark stepped up to the plate and hit a rocket, a base hit right up the middle. "He took that wide turn at 4.2 flat!" Freddie said. "Whew! This boy can run! This is my man! Let's go." He hadn't even looked at the rest of his tools.

"Freddie, you haven't even looked at Tony Gwynn yet." So I kidded him, "Freddie, you know you're cheating, and you know you don't wanna pay nothing." I said, "Now look, you can get Mark, but it's going to cost a hundred thousand dollars tax-free. That's what he wants. Are you willing to pay that? If you are, then I will take you up to the house and introduce you to his dad and you can do it." The Cards ended up drafting him in the fifth round.

Then we went over to San Diego State to see them play Cal State-Fullerton and he asked me, "Who do you think is the best player on the San Diego State team?"

I said, "Without a doubt, Tony Gwynn." So Angel, this rival scout, turned around and said to me, and I will never forget Angel saying this to me, he said, "Bull----." And Freddie gave him a long, stern look.

Finally, Freddie pointed his finger right in Angel's face and said, "Look, let me tell you something. I was not talking to you. You're sitting in front of us talking to someone else, so you talk to him. When I want your advice, I'll ask you for it." I always respected Freddie for this because he was talking to me, trying to find out what I thought and I told him. Tony Gwynn was the absolute best out there.

So then Freddie says to me, "Why do you think he's the best?" At that time he couldn't throw from left field to third base, but the kid could really hit and he could run the bases. His speed shocked me. And we talked about him a little while, and I told Freddie I thought he was a real hard worker before the games and you could see his determination out there. He wasn't pushing it. I don't mean that, because he was graceful.

I told Freddie, "Because of what he can do with that bat and because of all the work he does on his own time to improve the things he can't do as well as hit."

Now, Bobby Meacham was on that same team and he's the one the Cardinals took first that year. So when the game started, Meacham got a base on balls. Al Newman, who later went with the Minnesota Twins, was the number two hitter. Newman struck out. Tony Gwynn came up and hit a rocket right out of the ballpark. The second time up yet another rocket out of the park that hit a telephone pole. "See, Freddie, that's why I like him. He's my number one man."

So then Freddie began to trust my judgment better.

—Scout **Cecil Espy** in the book *Eye for Talent*

When you're a .330 something lifetime hitter you don't get mad very often, but he would get disgusted with himself more than anything. If he got in a little rut and he was trying to get out of it he would get frustrated. It wouldn't be a major snap. He was a professional all the way. Even those times when he was on the DL, he'd be in helping us do something in the clubhouse. We used to have to paint the brown shoes back in the early days and he'd be in helping mask off the stripes of whatever shoe company it was. He'd do everything. Make rosin bags...it didn't matter. No other player did that. He was the only player I've ever seen polish his own shoes. He'd tell my shoe boys, "I've got them. Don't worry."

We had an off day in Cincinnati years and years ago. I arranged the bus so that the coaching staff and myself could go down and check out Louisville Slugger. I was trying to get the players to join in, but I think he might've been one of the only players to take that trip with us. He got to know the factory guys turning the lathe which really helped, because as personal as he was, he talked to those guys while we were there, and the bats he got after that were incredible. He liked the wider grain bats and out of the dozen bats that we got there might've been one that had a thinner grain. The bats he got were unbelievable. When we were in **CINCINNATI***, Charlotte Jones and Chuck Shupp would come up from Louisville Slugger. He loved Charlotte. He was her boy and she took care of him. That was just Tony being Tony. He was just so personable to everybody.

The last time I saw Tony was at Jerry Coleman's memorial service here in town and I knew he was in trouble. He was still upbeat, he was Tony, but he didn't look right. We were on the road in Seattle when I heard that he had passed. I remember getting up that morning and I had a text message from the front office. It was a very sad day. He had that incredible, infectious laugh that we still hear. That's what John Boggs and I were talking about at his service. How his laugh would get you going. One of my favorite memories was the time up in Montreal when he got his 3,000th hit and he had all his family with him. That was a pretty special moment. And of course when he was inducted into the baseball Hall of Fame. I was fortunate enough to attend that.

—**Brian Prilaman**, Padres Equipment Manager

*Pete Rose is in the Summit County, Ohio Boxing Hall of Fame....In 1998 the **CINCINNATI** Reds started an outfield trio of Chris Stynes, Dimitri Young, and Mike Frank. You might know them better as Young, Frank, and Stynes. (The author couldn't resist. He'll show himself to the principal's office now.)

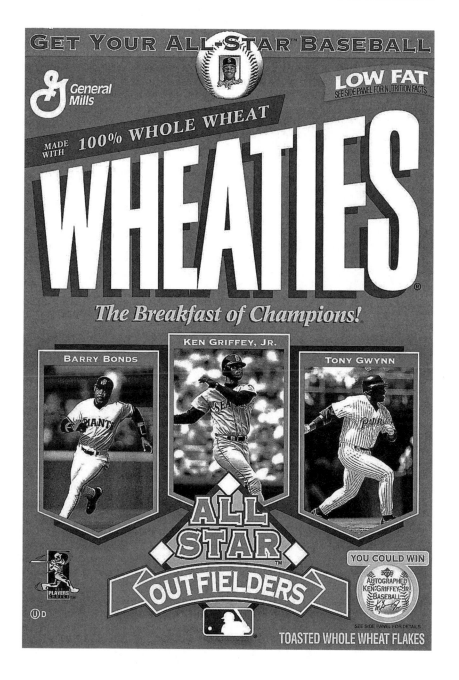

Tony Gwynn looks at a statue that was unveiled at Petco Park of Mr. Padre.

Chapter Four

THE WRITE STUFF

The Fourth Estate
Doesn't Take the Fifth

THE WRITE GUY

TOM KRASOVIC

Tom Krasovic writes NFL/Chargers commentary and reports on the Chargers. His football writings have appeared at ESPN. com, USA Today, *CBSSports.com and AOL. com. Tom worked for AOL FanHouse, the* Los Angeles Times, *the* Riverside Press-Enterprise *and* Aviation Week & Space Technology *magazine. He is a graduate of San Diego State.*

I was a baseball fanatic, and was so happy as a student at San Diego State to be able to watch the caliber of play. I'd skip class now and then to go and watch baseball at Smith Field, Jim Dietz's team. The best player on the team was named Gwynn, but it was **CHRIS GWYNN***. Tony had graduated by the time I was there. There's no question, Chris was the better college player, as good as Tony was. Now, remember Tony had also played basketball, so that may have slowed his baseball development a little bit. Chris was tremendous. He had the inside out swing. He had a lot more power, he ran well, and he just hit the daylights out of the ball. Chris was a first-round pick for the Dodgers, whereas Tony was a third-round pick for the Padres. Just an incredible amount of talent those two guys had in how they'd go about hitting the baseball, running the bases, anticipating, being smart, and playing the fundamentals. All of those things you always hear about.

*Tony Gwynn's brother **CHRIS** was an All-American baseball player at San Diego State. He played on the 1984 U.S. Olympic baseball team and was a first-round draft pick of the Los Angeles Dodgers. Another brother of Tony, Charles, was a baseball standout at Cal State-LA, and is now teaching in South Central Los Angeles.

I first knew Tony Gwynn in 1983 as a very young writer for the San Diego Union, where on occasion I would be required to get quotes down in the locker room. That was his second year with the Padres and my main memory from that time was that he was incredibly gracious. He was very bubbly, he was happy, and he enjoyed talking. The first time I met him when I became a beat writer was spring training of '95. He told me he had helped out Buster Olney and others who had preceded me on the beat and went on to bigger and better things. If I wanted to go on to bigger and better things, he would be glad to help. That's really unusual.

The Padres were a decent team that year. He thought they could be doing a little better and later in the season, he urged me to be more critical of the team when I wrote about them, because he felt like they were fading down the stretch. He didn't detail exactly why he wanted me to be more critical but he thought they needed someone else on the outside to motivate them. I've written NFL and college stories, but I've never had an athlete urging me to be more critical of the team.

I didn't always take his advice. But a day or two later the team had a horrible game and Tony came up to me and asked, "Do you think that was good baseball? Do you think that was crisp? You should whip us." I wrote a critical piece, he seemed to like the fact that I met his standards. He gave me a fist bump and congratulated me for handling the team. I can assure you I've never had that happen. I do recall the general manager, Randy Smith, being pretty angry about some of the things I had written.

That was Tony. I know you hear all about this stuff—and it's true—about the laugh and the kind of person that he was, but he certainly had an edge to him. Maybe more than people realize. He was very competitive and very candid. In 1998, when the team had a division clinching victory, everyone was celebrating, spraying champagne, and even though it was just a division title they went bonkers. The exception was Tony Gwynn. The next day I asked him why he had not taken part.

Well, on the record, he goes on a rant to me basically to the effect that the Padres hadn't won anything, and that if they got booted out of the playoffs like they did last time they went, he was going to blast them in the paper, and go off on them. Because in '96, they had lost in the first round by a sweep to the **CARDINALS***. He didn't want one and done.

When I wrote what he had to say—and he had gone on pretty good about it—the front office was really angry at him. The manager, Bruce Bochy, was mad at him and a few of the players were very angry at his rant, because Tony rained on their parade. I was a little bit apprehensive about how he was going to react. A lot of times with athletes, when it comes out in a paper, it has a different effect than they had hoped. But he was perfectly fine with it. He actually enjoyed it, he liked it. He didn't mind at all that they were upset at him. And, as you know, they went down to the Yankees in the World Series. That story adds a little depth to his true legacy. He was an incredible hitter and a very good person, but he was very serious and determined. I agreed with him on his criticism of that celebration when they won the division. I agreed with him most all the time.

I think that if Tony had kept his **WEIGHT DOWN*** he would've caught Pete Rose for most hits. I say that with great humility because the record that Rose set is truly mind-boggling. Rose

---

*All six games of the 1944 World Series were played at Sportsman's Park in St. Louis. The rival managers—Luke Sewell of the Browns and Billy Southworth of the **CARDINALS**—shared a one-bedroom apartment... never expecting that both teams would be in town at the same time.

---

*In 2009, Gwynn had a lap-band procedure on his stomach in order to lose **WEIGHT**. He had ballooned to 330 pounds, 100 pounds more than when he played. He lost weight at first, and then stopped following the diet, which contributed to severe back pains that created a slipped disc which affected a nerve in his lower leg. He needed a walker to get around at that time.

was a force of nature, even if he was a force of nature on amphetamines. You know the story of how Rose would pass around amphetamines in a jar before the game. To achieve what Rose achieved, the man was consumed by competition.

To say anyone could have matched that is very bold, but I think Tony's weight was the obstacle. It wasn't the hand-eye coordination, or the love of baseball, or the hitting. He would never get bored with this stuff which is truly incredible. He was very diligent about this preparation. The obstacle was the health of his legs. His legs kept breaking down on him. The people I've talked to in the sports medical community will tell you this, on a baseball player mere pounds—one, two, three, four pounds—are significant as it plays out over a season with the workload and the stress load. It's very difficult to do but if he had stayed at the same playing weight as he had early in his career, I think he would have really challenged Pete Rose's hitting record.

Jerry Coleman used to tell me that his weight remained constant from the time he joined the New York Yankees to close to the end of his life. If Tony had that kind of constant weight from the early '80s onward maybe you could tack on five years and 900 hits. It would still leave him short, but... Maybe instead of tacking on five years, he'd have had three full years towards the end instead of three compromised years.

When I first saw Gwynn back in '83, Tony could really run. He could really run. He was quick. I wouldn't say he was what the scouts call an 80 runner, but he was a 65 runner on the 1 to 80 scale that the scouts use. He told me he was 5 foot 9½ in reality. He could dunk a basketball at that height. He had small hands, so he had to dunk that ball either with two hands or use centrifugal force to get it up there. He was really athletic.

The happiest I ever saw him was when his brother Chris in '96 basically won the National League West against the Los Angeles Dodgers by doubling off Chan Ho Park at Dodger Stadium to break it open late in a very low scoring game. The Padres were able to celebrate winning the National League West title for the first time in 12 years. Oh my goodness, I've never seen him happier than after his brother came through for the team. He loved his brother and his brother is such a good guy. Chris had had a miserable year, statistically terrible. Chris was a pinch-hitter and pinch-hitting is very, very hard. Everyone understands that you could be hitting .180 as a pinch-hitter and that's not a huge deal because you get so few chances to play. I think Tony sensed that people believed Chris was on the team because his last name was Gwynn, and here when he came up with this hit, it just opened the floodgates. He was so excited. I can still see him in that very small clubhouse at Dodger Stadium and he's hugging everybody, he's hugging reporters. I've never seen him happier than that.

The other time I saw him when he was really happy was Game 1 of the '98 World Series at Yankee Stadium. He could not sit still. He was bouncing up-and-down. He almost hit his head on the dugout a few times. He just held court there for hours. He was like a greeter sitting in the dugout. Whoever came by, he would smile and shout out their name, and tell them stories. You just haven't seen anyone more excited for something, other than maybe children on Christmas Day. That really is how he was. Tony was so excited about Bob Sheppard, the legendary **YANKEE P.A. ANNOUNCER***, saying his name. Watching him I thought to myself that he really deserves this. It's one of those things where he knew how great this was and he was going to enjoy every moment of it. Then when the game began, he just flipped on that switch, he was so ready and he was real comfortable. He had an excellent game that day and he had an excellent World Series.

*The **PUBLIC ADDRESS ANNOUNCER** for the Houston Colt '45s (later the Astros) in their 1962 inaugural season was Dan Rather...the P.A. announcer for the Brooklyn Dodgers in 1936 and 1937 was John Forsythe, later a TV and movie star.

A side story to that one is that his wife and son, who was 16 at the time, were sitting in the VIP section at Yankee Stadium, and Denzel Washington and Bruce Willis were there. They're Yankee fans and they were teasing Junior during the game. Junior is a very polite young man and mom is the disciplinarian, so they didn't have much to say. When dad hit the home run, Junior jumped to his feet and let them have it. He told them, "Take that," as his dad trotted around the bases. I guess Alicia was mortified momentarily at how her son was behaving. It was a great memory for the whole family.

Tony could really blow up, but it never was something that lingered with him. The maddest I saw him was after my newspaper assigned me a story to write about his weight, which most people didn't like to write about for good reason. He had gotten wind of it; that I was talking to other people before I talked to him. We were in **FULTON COUNTY STADIUM*** in Atlanta in the dugout one-on-one, and he just went off. He said, "I've heard you've been asking about my weight." He didn't like that subject one bit, and he let me know about it at length. He was livid.

When we ran that story—and the story wasn't too bad—but unbeknownst to me the paper had put together a chart, charting his year-by-year weight—and that set him off again. When I got to the clubhouse the next day, he was even angrier than he was in Atlanta. And he let me have it there. That put me in the position of trying to say that I didn't know that the chart was coming, but that's not a good thing to say because it makes you look like you're making excuses about your own paper. So that's an example of where I know he was very mad.

One time at Qualcomm, we were sitting in the dugout well before a game. Some guy leaned over the rail and interrupted

*Ted Turner once managed his Atlanta Braves. Baseball Commissioner Bowie Kuhn put a stop to it after one game...Until the Colorado Rockies debuted in the early 90s, ATLANTA had the highest elevation of any major league team.

him a couple of times asking him to sign a ball. The guy would not wait. He was very impatient. Tony had asked him to wait because he was in the middle of a conversation. The guy kept after him and Tony just went ballistic on him. It was very funny, in a way. The guy had it coming to a point, but I think Tony had a whole lot of stress on him and he discharged a whole lot of it in this one episode.

I knew Gwynn for 31 years. I was one of the crazy ones, I used to cover Padres baseball five months a year. I covered six weeks of spring training and seventy-five road games, and I did all the home games. I talked to him an awful lot. You have to remember this guy gave more interviews in a season than a football player does in his whole career. Not just chit-chat or talking about himself. There's no doubt that Tony Gwynn was the number one sports figure in San Diego. No disrespect to the other great ones, like Junior Seau and Lance Alworth. People really can't comprehend what an ambassador he was for the city and the sport. They don't get it.

> There's no doubt that Tony Gwynn was the number one sports figure in San Diego.

Bud Selig doesn't understand it. He wasn't even at the memorial service, which was a huge mistake. Then, MLB didn't even do anything at the All-Star Game. Those are two examples of the people in MLB making millions of dollars a year, where guys like Tony Gwynn played a big role in him bringing in that kind of salary. They still don't get it.

The whole 2014 Fox All-Star Game was ridiculous. MLB just glossed over Tony Gwynn. Selig sent Rob Manfred out for the memorial and it was a very perfunctory effort on his part. Again, I don't know what Bud was doing at that time, but unless it was a very, very important thing that I frankly can't think of off the top of my head, Tony Gwynn embodied everything that Bud Selig purports to embody. A small media market team that went to two World Series, which is pretty good, a great ambassador for the game. Another reason to celebrate him—no hint of drug use!

In the late 90s, I wrote about Kevin Towers, the general manager, and Bruce Bochy, the manager of the Padres both trying to quit dipping tobacco. As somebody who didn't smoke or chew tobacco myself I was a little surprised to find out what a terribly addicting habit it is...that chewing tobacco was worse than smoking cigarettes, which is awfully tough to kick on its own. Then, a year two later I'd see the two of them still dipping. Those experiences gave me—I can't say it was a sense of foreboding—but certainly a sense of unease and sadness that it was such an awful habit to kick.

We'd write about **JOE GARAGIOLA SR.*** periodically, and Joe was a strong advocate for baseball to speak out and legislate against tobacco use in the minor leagues. Joe's speeches and his graphic displays were very powerful in showing what tobacco can do to your mouth and your face. That it was cancerous. But I didn't connect those dots with Tony until he had that fourteen-hour surgery. Thereafter, I wrote a couple of stories, including one for a local magazine, talking to him and his family about it. At the time, the hope was that they had gotten all of it. What an ordeal to go through and the hope was that it wouldn't take his life.

On the day he died, I was at home. My boss called me, and at that point I thought he misdialed, because he started talking about "could I help out on the 'Gwynn thing,'" I said, "What Gwynn thing?" And he just floored me.

It was very emotional. My wife ran into his wife at a restaurant recently and you just can't imagine what she's going through, because that guy really was a force of nature and had such a presence to him. It's a void, a huge void.

*Joe **GARAGIOLA**'s wife, Audrey, was at one time the organist at Sportsman's Park, in St. Louis when Garagiola played for the Cardinals.

He was very comfortable in San Diego. He could've gotten millions more elsewhere, but he was comfortable here. He was smart too, he was astute. He realized that there would be a dividend to staying with the Padres down the road. He ended up becoming a paid consultant to the team. He became coach of his alma mater, he got to see his son and coach his son and daughter. He and his wife have family in Long Beach.

> He could've gotten millions more elsewhere, but he was comfortable here.

Basically, that's it. They did go to two World Series. We know how the baseball economics are. We know the Padres were terrible for a number years when he was here, but it wasn't the outpost necessarily at times that people think. There are a lot of great baseball players who played a lot of years and didn't go to one World Series. I know he did play for twenty years, but he did get to go to two, and a third playoff.

A lot of us in the media didn't go to his Hall of Fame induction for a variety of reasons. He wanted to have a night with us, so he rented out a suite at the ballpark with food and drink, and we all spent a few hours there talking with him about what it was going to be like to go to the Hall of Fame, and revisiting his whole career.

That's the kind of guy he was, though. He wanted to make sure all of us got a chance to be part of it too, even though we weren't going. We had a great three hours or so with him at the ballpark, which was always easy to do with him. That was my memory of his Hall of Fame induction. That was before he went to Cooperstown, and it allowed us to write a lot of the extra stories leading up to it, which was great.

I didn't see much of Tony at San Diego State. Where I would see him was at the park while he was working with ESPN and with the Padres broadcast team. That was always fun, 'cause he'd swing by the press box about three or four hours before the game, or I would go by the booth. We'd talk about the last night's game, and talk about what's happening in MLB. He loved to talk basketball. He was a big fan of the Indiana Pacers, because he had a home in **INDIANAPOLIS*** where he'd spend part of the winter.

He liked that Indy was low-key. It's sort of reflected his personality. He liked that it was different and he loved basketball. He fell in love with the Pacers. I know he liked watching them. He was a Midwest guy in a way. He was plain-spoken, direct, unassuming, and that's the kind of place that the Midwest is. He liked the open space, it was different from Long Beach, different from Poway. When the Padres were playing the Reds, he'd go there and spend the night at his home in Indianapolis. He really looked forward to being there.

Tony was such a good hitter, and he made it look so simple. And then the way he handled himself off the field was off the charts.

He was a fine, fine man!

*The 1955 NBA Finals were played in Indianapolis even though **INDIANAPOLIS** did not have an NBA team until 1976. The Fort Wayne Zollner Pistons' arena was booked so Fort Wayne—now the Detroit Pistons—had to find an alternate site.

ARE YOU NOW OR HAVE YOU EVER BEEN A COLUMNIST?

NICK CANEPA

Senior sports columnist Nick Canepa, a native San Diegan, graduated from San Diego State and began working for the U-T in 1971. He joined the sports department in 1974 and covered high schools, SDSU athletics, the Clippers, the Chargers, wrote a TV-radio column and became a general sports columnist in 1984. He has covered nearly every major sporting event in the world.

Tony didn't start on the basketball team his freshman year, but he played a lot. That was an all-white team. They used to call them the White Tornado…an all-white starting five. Then Tony started his last three years and he played baseball after his freshman year. My one year covering the Clippers was right after Tony left school in '81. The Clippers drafted him. Tony would have started on that Clippers team. They were awful. John Douglas was their point guard and Tony was a much better player than John Douglas. A much better passer. I'd wager right now that Tony Gwynn would have led the **NBA IN ASSISTS*** his first year in the league. I would bet everything I own on it. Michael Brooks who was a phenomenal player was always the first guy down the court for the Clippers and nobody could get the ball to him. Well, Tony would have got the ball to him. He was a decent shooter, a good ball handler, and a great passer.

*Ernie DiGregorio led the **NBA** in assists as a rookie with the Buffalo Braves in the 1970s. His dad was the official scorer. The Buffalo Braves later became the San Diego Clippers.

Tony was always open and honest. They weren't all that good his senior year and Smokey Gaines was coaching the team then. Smokey and Tony didn't have the greatest of relationships. Smokey had his own ideas and I'm sure Tony had his and it wasn't that they were always arguing but it was like oil and water. They weren't best of friends, let's put it that way. Anyway, one night they played Texas El Paso. Tony hit a 55-foot shot right at the buzzer that would have tied the game but the refs waived it off.

Smokey went nuts. They ruled he shot it after the buzzer. Everybody's going crazy and Tony said "Yeah, it was after the buzzer. I didn't make the shot. I didn't get it off in time." Most athletes in that situation would probably say they made it. Tony was different than most athletes. I thought he was right but Smokey made a big stink about it and fans were going crazy. You know how fans are.

The Aztecs used to get 2,000 fans a game if they were lucky. That's a lot. Three really good players and an assistant coach from Tony's one team at SDSU have already passed. Hard to believe!

When they went back to Yankee Stadium for the first time for the '98 World Series he was happy being around that place and all the legends. He was always happy. When you asked Vin Scully to describe Tony Gwynn he said one word: Jolly. Tony was always in a good mood. One year he stole over 50 bases. Look at Tony later in his career and you say "how did he even move?" But Tony was a great athlete. The one thing that always sticks out to me more than anything is his home run off the Bud Light sign in Yankee Stadium in the first game of the '98 World Series. It was the hardest ball I ever saw him hit, and I saw him hit a lot of balls. That thing just ricocheted off the second deck. He kind of pooh-poohed it later on. Later he admitted it was his favorite hit. He knocked the hell out of that ball.

Tony wasn't one of those guys who hid from the media in the training room. Dr. J was also good with the media. I was there when the 76ers lost to the Lakers in Los Angeles and the last guy in the locker room was Dr. J. When you get guys like that, especially with the young guys coming up, they feed off that. I remember walking through the Marriott at the L.A airport and Dr. J was singing with this group in the middle of the lobby. They'd just lost. That's the way Tony was. Tony never hid. I know what idiots baseball writers are...I'm one of them...but Tony endeared himself to these guys. Here's a big-time National League batting champion who was always there for people and there's just not many of those guys. When writers came from out of town and said "I'm so and so from Cincinnati," Tony said, "How are you doing?" He was always available.

Tony Gwynn is at the top of the hundreds of athletes I've dealt with. There are a lot of good ones certainly. San Diego has Phillip Rivers now. He's just tremendous. He's a talking machine. He's as good as anybody but he hasn't been around for 20 years like Tony. Whenever you need something, he's there. That's the way Tony was. He was a pioneer. I remember going over to Yuma when he was still a kid and going to his room. He was playing a video game.

One time...my kids were little...we went to Yuma. My youngest son was really little. I took my sons John and Anthony over to the field and we were standing outside the clubhouse. I introduced Tony to the kids and he said, "Just a minute." Tony went inside and came back and gave them both a bat. The kids were thrilled. Another time, he looks at me and says "Where'd you get those sunglasses?" I said, "My good ones broke." He said, "Man, those are terrible, awful." I said, "Ah, they're just cheap things because I lost my good ones." He says, "Just a minute." Tony goes into the clubhouse and he comes out with a pair of Oakleys. He gave me a pair of Oakleys. He had just signed a deal with Oakley. He had started wearing sunglasses at the plate, remember? And a lot of people weren't doing that then. He started wearing them because it helped him. Whatever he could do to improve himself he did. He felt comfortable with them.

When he came up, Tony was in as tough a clubhouse as you can be in. Baseball's changed dramatically in the last 30 years. Baseball players are much easier to get along with now than they used to be. When Tony came up, that locker room with Craig Nettles and Goose Gossage was a tough locker room... a very veteran locker room. They had Garvey in there, "Mr. Nice Guy." Barry Bloom, the beat guy, covered the Padres for us during that period...almost the entire team wouldn't talk to him. I think that included the manager, **DICK WILLIAMS***. But Tony and Garvey did.

Players are a lot better now than they used to be. I don't know why. The Chargers were a very veteran team in the early '80s. And Dan Fouts is as tough a guy as you'll ever meet in your life. It's just the way they were. They're different now, but they're not Tony Gwynn.

Fouts used to run around with that MFIC hat on. I don't think anyone got along with him among the writers better than me and he was a pain in the neck....after games you could hardly talk to him. They could win by 50 and he was still a PITA. He's still not "Mr. Nice Guy." Dan's Dan. He's a competitive son of a gun. He was something. Wow. Talk about fire. That guy had fire.

Chuck Muncie was a good guy. Screwed up but he was a great guy. Joe "Jelly Bean" Bryant was a good guy. Kobe's father. He was basically a head case. You never knew what you were going to get from him from one day to the next, but I thought he was great. I've always gotten along great with Phil Mickleson. I've known him since he was a teenager. Phil's uncle, Tony, through marriage, was my best friend in high school.

About 25 years ago, we set up a photo shoot with Tony. We lit a

---

*In the "Jackie Robinson Story", **DICK WILLIAMS** (later a Padres and Hall of Fame manager) was an extra. In one scene Williams is pitching for Jersey City when Robinson homers for Montreal...When Robinson nears second base on his home run trot, the second baseman is Dick Williams.

bat on fire with lighter fluid and got a picture of him swinging that bat on fire. He gave me that bat....Is there anybody in history who signed more autographs than Tony Gwynn? Probably not. His autograph may not be worth five cents a thousand years from now.

There will never be another one like him. We'll have great players here, but I don't know if we'll have another Tony Gwynn. I can't imagine that happening.

He treated everybody great. He always had time for you. Even when he didn't have time for you, he had time for you. I never saw him turn anybody away. I know there were times when he didn't want to talk about something. I'd have some idea about something, and he'd say, "Ah, I don't want to talk about that." That's just the way he was.

I covered Tony from the day he stepped on the campus in 1977. I was Aztec beat writer then. He just played basketball his freshman year, because Tim Vezie, the coach then, wouldn't allow him to play baseball.

I think it was Tony's second to the last game, his senior year, and they played El Paso here, UTEP, and UTEP was really good. San Diego State wasn't very good, but they played them tough, and it was a two-point game,—this was before the three-point shot—Gwynn came down the court with time running out and launched a fifty-plus-foot shot, and nailed it. Just nailed it. The refs waived it off, said it came after the buzzer.

Well Smokey Gaines was coach then and he goes completely nuts. Screaming, you know. So I go up to Tony, and Tony said, "I didn't beat the buzzer." His coach is going crazy saying he did and Tony said, "Nah, I didn't beat the buzzer." And that was Tony.

He was unique. He was brilliant. Tony got it. A lot of guys don't get it, and still don't get it. He knew more than...You can go around baseball now and find locker rooms, full locker rooms that don't know as much as he knew. He was a brilliant guy.

TONY GWYNN'S MEMORIES ARE FREE...AND WORTH EVERY PENNY

CHRIS JENKINS

Chris Jenkins has been the Major League Baseball writer for the U-T since 1999, covering the Padres on a regular basis for the past five years. Early in his career as a journalistic jack-of-all-sports, Jenkins covered the "Miracle on Ice" in Lake Placid for the Colorado Springs Gazette-Telegraph. Since coming to the U-T in 1982, he's worked five Winter and five Summer Olympics, filed datelines from four continents and Cuba, written about sporting events as wide-ranging as rodeos and bonspiels, covered Super Bowls, Final Fours and NBA Finals.

There are "go to guys," and then there are guys that you almost have to push yourself not to go to them because you go to them so often. Tony was not only brilliant in terms of baseball analysis and all that, but he was also happily willing to share his input.

He believed that the more you knew about the game and what had gone on, the better off our readers were, the better off everyone was. I can't remember Tony ever holding too much of anything back, unlike most ball players who get really, really defensive and really protective. When you walk into the locker room with Tony, the problem was it was too good. You couldn't write about Tony every day. You could have, but the readers would go, "Wait a minute. What is this?"

So, there were times, once or twice a week, when I would go into the Padres locker room and I'd make a point of not even looking to the right, which was where his locker was. Because

I knew if I made eye contact with him, I'd be over there for the next 45 minutes, learning everything he wanted to share about last night's game, or whatever. He was wonderful, he was absolutely wonderful. If Tony was a guy pumping gas, or a surgeon, or whatever, he would still have been one in a million.

There's got to be some genetics involved in making him that way because every Gwynn I've met has been exactly the same. His brother, Chris Gwynn, is an extremely nice and intelligent person. And Tony Gwynn Jr. is his father's son. They even sound alike, their voices are identical.

Tony could've handled New York, but I'm not sure he wanted to handle New York. Certainly, he could've played for the Dodgers, they were the team of his youth. He was a family man, who found a place where he loved raising his family. He would have loved to have been in more World Series, but he found a home when he was 18 years old when he came to college.

Probably the happiest I ever saw him was when he was with Tony Jr. in the dugout. As great as he was at what he did, I remember seeing him a hundred times being in the dugout hours before games, and **TONY JR.*** would be 14 years old in a uniform. Just the two of them together, just a father and son hanging out. Just quality time. That was the happiest I've ever seen Tony.

I miss everything about him, just everything. When you were with him, you felt like you were with one of those special people on the planet. He was great, he was great in every respect.

One of the many amazing things about Tony was his ability to not get stumped by anybody. You could see it in the way pitchers were always trying to challenge Tony. Always trying to

***TONY GWYNN JR.**'s first Major League hit on July 19, 2006 came 24 years to the day after his father's first Major League hit. Both hits were doubles.

figure out some way to get the ball past him...trying to fool him. You could not fool Tony Gwynn. You couldn't surprise him in any way. I don't know if the guy was ever surprised by anything in his life.

Well, we had the same challenge as writers who spent a lot of time around Tony. So, the challenge became to ask a question where Tony went "I don't know. I don't know. You stumped me." And my first question was, "Tony, so what do you think of the new Clinton tax plan."

Immediately, like that, Tony goes, "Ah, man, my dad and I were just talking about this last night. My dad said 'We need to tax the corporations more. We need to tax the corporations more.' And I said, 'Dad, I am a corporation.'"

It strikes me, now that I've been thinking back to these kinds of stories. I wish more corporations were like Tony. I wish they had learned something from a corporation like Tony on how to treat people.

It's one thing to watch a guy hit an incredible home run at Yankee Stadium in front of seventy thousand people and a national audience. But the good stuff was when it was just you and him, and you were just talking, and he just enthralled you with his personality, and with his kindness.

He used to love to stump us. We'd sit down with him and Tony would go, "So, **BARRY BONDS***, Hall-of-Fame?" And I'd go, "Ah, Tony, I don't know, I got the vote, but I don't know if I can bring myself to do it." And Tony would go, "How could you not put Barry Bonds in? How can you not do that? I mean, look at his numbers. Look what he's done. Look what he did before all this. How could you not..."

---

*In 2002 **B*RRY B*NDS** received 68 intentional walks...Eight came when no one was on base.

All of a sudden you're like, "Holy smokes." And you're backing up from the guy. And that's the way he wanted. That's exactly the way he wanted it.

I went into the Pittsburgh Pirates locker room. I went up to Andrew McCutchen, the reigning Most Valuable Player. Andrew is only in his mid-twenties. I dropped the name Tony Gwynn. I asked him, "What can you tell me about Tony Gwynn?"

He said, "Honestly, I can't say I saw him play a lot. I grew up in Florida. I was really young when he was playing, but I know about the video, I know about the video." And at that point he pointed over to the middle of the visiting locker room at Petco. There was a bank of about five or six laptops there, and there was a player in front of every laptop sitting there, clicking, clicking, clicking, and studying that day's pitcher.

McCutchen said, "He started that. Gwynn was the guy who taught everybody how to make yourself better. How to show somebody the little things, or even the big things that you can do to make yourself better."

The year Tony Gwynn last played with the Padres, I had a meeting in Houston. As it turned out the Padres were playing the Astros, so, of course, I went to the game and wore my Padres ball cap. No fewer than 40 people came up to me at the game and said the only reason they were at the game was to see Tony Gwynn.

—**Mike Maier**, Del Mar

LET'S GET TECHNICAL, TECHNICAL

MICHAEL SCHELL

In 1999, Michael Schell wrote Baseball's All-Time Best Hitters. *Using a combination of statistics and analysis, Schell proclaimed that Tony Gwynn was the greatest hitter in the history of Major League Baseball.*

My brothers and I wanted to play fantasy baseball with players from all different time periods. To do that you can't take their averages from the back of the baseball cards and translate from one era to another. So I had to adjust for a number of different factors to do that properly and this required some statistics work. What it comes down to, is how much better are players than the peers they're playing with, and how do you make sure that you're fair when comparing players that played 100 years ago to players who played 10 years ago or today.

You can look at how well one player compares to other players and there were two adjustments that deal with that. It turns out also that the ballpark where the player plays makes a difference and you need to account for that factor. When the Rockies play at a **MILE HIGH*** in Colorado, the ball travels about 19 feet farther than it does at sea level. That makes it easier for players to hit the ball more often and farther. Fans know this too. In fact one year, when Tony Gwynn was in a battle with Dante Bichette for who would have the highest batting average by the most number of hits per at-bat, and the Rockies came to San

*In the upper deck at Coors Field in Denver, there is a row of seats painted purple all the way around the stadium to signify the **MILE-HIGH** altitude level.

Diego, fans at San Diego held up a sign saying, "Welcome to sea level" to point out that Dante Bichette's hits were easier to come by because of where he played. So, you have to adjust for that in order to make it fair.

The last adjustment is for players who have very long careers. During their final playing years, they tend not to hit as well as they did it earlier in their careers. My job was to find out who was the best during the prime of their career, so I tracked their numbers for the first 8,000 times they got an at-bat. When I crunched all those numbers in 1997, Tony Gwynn, who was still playing at the time, looked as if he was the best of all time over a hundred years of baseball play. Before Gwynn came along, the player who held that spot retired in 1927. That was Ty Cobb. What was happening in 1997 was that we were seeing a player currently playing who looked as if he was the best at excelling past his peers since Ty Cobb retired. Ty Cobb is often thought of as the best hitter of all time because his lifetime batting average is .367.

I believe Tony Gwynn's average is .338. If you just look at hits and at-bats straight up, it looks like Tony Gwynn is 18th best hitter all time. But that didn't account for all the other adjustments you need to make—the time period or era the player played, the ballpark they played in. When you make those adjustments, it turns out that in fact Tony Gwynn was better for average than Ty Cobb.

During the 1997 season, I traveled out to San Diego to talk to Tony Gwynn on the occasion of his 8,000th at-bat, the last at-bat that would count for him to qualify for my calculations. On that occasion, he was on the cover of both the *Sporting News* and **SPORTS ILLUSTRATED**.* The headline in *Sports Illustrated* called

*In 1955, **SPORTS ILLUSTRATED** selected horse owner William Woodward as their Sportsman of the Year. Woodward's wife shot and killed the unfaithful Woodward before the issue went to press. S.I. then selected World Series hero, Johnny Podres.

Tony the greatest hitter since Ted Williams. I was out there to tell him that he was the greatest hitter in spite of Ted Williams or Ty Cobb. They did an adjustment, but they only did one adjustment not the four that I did.

Tony Gwynn knew what I had done because I had sent out a press release about this earlier. The Padres allowed me to come to the game early and go in the dugout. I was there in the dugout and Tony walked by right in front of me, so I said, "Tony, I'm Michael Schell." He said, "So you're the guy. You're putting pressure on me." I said, "You're getting no pressure from me. You've already done it." He already had the clinching hit about two weeks earlier and I was there to celebrate with him the fact that I believed he was the greatest hitter for average that the game has ever produced. I said, "I'm here because I believe you're the best at doing this." He said, "I really appreciate that and I've got something for you."

He left and then the Padres management called me up into the locker room. Tony gave me a signed bat, wristbands, and batting gloves that he had. The signed bat that he gave me was a bat that he had used in play that year, which is very unusual for players to do that. Often times, players are very superstitious and they don't want to give up bats they use in games. I got a picture with him and I really enjoyed that moment. I was very surprised at how down to earth he was. I had met a few other players while I was going through this process of calculating the best player of all time, and they just didn't have that same personality that Tony did. He was very humble and that made the whole experience more enjoyable for me.

It was really special that he gave me one of his game-used bats. He told me, "There're hits on this bat." In fact, the bat he gave me had racing stripes around it, which I think he did himself. He could do that with his bats most likely because he didn't break his bats. Most times when you watch players now they break bats every couple of games. But Tony was noted for having a bat that he used all season without breaking it. He actually invested energy into the bat he gave me and that really showed me his generosity of spirit.

In the game today, the number of strikeouts the players make, have been going way up, and are still going up, from where they were 60 or 70 years ago. Tony struck out at an usually low amount for his era than any other player in the game's history.

Tony Gwynn had a good early part of his career but was still behind Ty Cobb. But he poured it on in the second part of his career when most players decline significantly. He just continued to play at a very high-level year after year. It only became clear in about '95 that this guy might be able to hold on long enough to surpass Ty Cobb. Ty Cobb was noted for the fact that he won 11 batting titles in 12 years. Tony Gwynn won eight but it's harder to win a batting title in the era Tony Gwynn played because there are twice as many players then there were in Cobb's time. There's a lot more competition today but Tony still won eight batting titles.

He was the greatest hitter ever and I proved it!

No drug scandals, no DUIs, no crazy nightclub fights, and his work ethic both on and off field was unmatched. Tony was much more than a ballplayer he was a righteous man. Heaven gained a good one.

—**Lance Jordan**, Bonita

Chapter Five

FRIAR LUCK

Padre Talk

TOO OLD TO BE YOUNG
TOO YOUNG TO BE OLD

JACK MCKEON

Better known as Trader Jack, Jack McKeon managed the Padres from '88 to '90. In 2003, as the manager of the Florida Marlins he became the oldest manager to win a World Series. John Aloysius McKeon was twice the National League Manager of the Year. He resides in Elon, North Carolina near his daughter and son-in-law, former Padre pitcher Greg Booker.

Back in 1981, San Diego State didn't have the restrictions on the number of games the team could play like they have today. They could play practically any time. They started playing probably on January 1. All the scouts would be in the ballpark every night watching Bobby Meacham, their star shortstop, play. I lived about two and half miles from the ballpark and I had nothing else to do, so I went over and watched them play as well.

In the meantime, February rolled on, March rolled on and we headed to spring training. We came back from spring training. Of course, you gotta remember too that the scouts had been watching Bobby Meacham for a month or so. Now they had to go out and look at other players. In the meantime, we didn't realize that Tony Gwynn wasn't playing because he was playing basketball. As many as 15 or 20 games that I'd seen San Diego State play, I never saw Tony Gwynn.

The Padres always played San Diego State in exhibition games before the season started and donated the receipts to the San Diego State baseball program. On this one particular night, I was sitting up in my box at the stadium and this guy Gwynn comes up and he triples off Steve Mura. Next time up, he doubles off Juan Eichelberger. These were two of my better pitchers and Tony didn't get lucky hits off them. When I saw how he hit the ball and his concentration, and how he ran the bases and the instincts he had, everything was coming together for me. I thought, "This is the guy, this is the guy."

I said to one of our scouts, "Who the heck is this guy?" He said, "That's Tony Gwynn." I said, "Where did he come from?" He said, "Well, he's only been playing for about a week. He's been playing basketball." I said, "Well, hell, he's the best player on this team." I went back to see him a couple more times, and was really impressed with his instincts. It was like he had eyes behind his head, and when he ran the bases he was very fluid, very smart, great instincts.

So now, here we come draft time. We bring a few of our cross-checkers in—some of our scouts—and we're discussing all these players. We are going to pick this guy McReynolds from Arkansas and he's going to be our number one pick and I said Tony Gwynn will be two. Then a few of our scouts said that they had this guy Billy Long out of **MIAMI OF OHIO***. I said to these guys, "I don't know. You've seen Tony Gwynn. You've seen Billy Long. Are you saying Billy Long is a better player than Tony Gwynn?" They said, "Yeah. Oh yeah." I said, "Well I'll go along with you. But regardless, Tony Gwynn is the next pick. There's no question." Well, we were very lucky that we got Billy Long in the second round and then we ended up getting Tony Gwynn in round 3.

We bring him in, we signed him for $25,000. He goes on to the rookie league up in Walla Walla, Washington. He's up there tearing the cover off the ball. He's leading the league in batting

---

***Do you confuse Miami (Ohio) with Miami (Florida)? MIAMI OF OHIO** was a school before Florida was a state.

average. That happened to be the strike year. The players were on strike. So I sent Clyde McCullough, the old veteran catcher from the Chicago Cubs, up to Walla Walla. He was the coach in the bullpen for us that year. We're paying them so since the players were on strike they had nothing to do.

A couple of weeks later, I flew up to Walla Walla to see our kids. On the team we had Tony Gwynn, John Kruk, Greg Booker, guys who eventually made the big leagues from that 1981 draft. I took the coaches and staff out to dinner one night and I asked them, "So, how many prospects do we have here?" One or two of the guys jumped up and said "Ah, we've only got one guy here." A guy named Louis Langie that we drafted in the sixth round. Clyde McCullough went crazy. He just jumped up "What the hell are you guys looking at here? There's at least three major league prospects on this team." He really ripped into those guys. He said, "We have Tony Gwynn and Greg Booker and John Kruk." Anyway, to make a long story short, Clyde had his piece to say and he ended up being right. The funny thing was Tony Gwynn was leading the league in hitting. I said to the manager, "Get him out of there. Move him up. He's too good for that league. Send him to AA." He ended up being Player of the Year in the Northwest League.

About the middle of November or something like that Sy Berger from **TOPPS*** Baseball Cards called me. He said, "Jack, I've got a problem." I asked him, "What's your problem, Sy?" He said, "I've got four or five of your scouts claiming Tony Gwynn." I laughed and said, "Let me go through the scouting files and see which guy should be credited." I went through the scouting files and there was one report on Tony Gwynn. That was from Cliff Ditto out of the Los Angeles area. That was the only scouting report we had. So I told Sy, "Make them all feel good. Give

---

*In the very first set of **TOPPS** baseball cards, the first card (#1) was Andy Pafko.

them all a certificate or whatever they need." They all claimed Tony Gwynn but we had only one report.

Tony went to spring training and he had a great spring down there. We had drafted Alan Wiggins out of the Dodger organization that year and we decided to send both him and Tony out to Hawaii. I told them to "go out there, bust your tail, do good, and if you're having a some success, and if we have an opportunity or an injury or something to bring you up, we'll do so."

Things were going pretty good until we had an injury. Well, Dick Williams was the manager and Dick wanted Tony Gwynn. I said, "You know, Dick, what kind of message are we sending to our players? Tony Gwynn was hitting about .239 at the time and Alan Wiggins was hitting about .319." I said, "That's not fair. I told both of those guys to go down and do the job and if you do the job we'll reward you. How can I take a guy hitting .239 to the big leagues and overlook the guy hitting .319?" I said, "I'll tell you what we'll do. We'll give Wiggins the first shot. We'll look at him for 30 days and if he doesn't do the job we'll go get Tony Gwynn. Okay, that was fine. Well, Wiggins came up and did a good job. We had another injury within about a month. By then, Tony Gwynn was hitting about .320. We bring Tony up. So now we got both of those guys starting their careers in the big leagues and having pretty good years.

When we brought Tony up from Hawaii, he probably couldn't throw as well as he needed to. He was that type of guy who spent a lot of time playing basketball and didn't have a very strong arm. But when you got to know Tony Gwynn, he had such a desire to become an All-Star. He wanted to be the best he could be, and this guy worked as hard as the most dedicated guy I've ever managed or been associated with. He made himself into a Hall of Famer. Clyde McCullough took him every night out to right field, took a dozen balls and had him pick up the ball and throw it all the way into second base. Clyde went out there and helped strengthen Tony's arm and he ended up being a Gold

Glove outfielder. Tony was determined he wanted to be a base stealer. He worked at that and had 56 stolen bases one year.

To me, Tony Gwynn is the father of the video in baseball. Today, organizations have multi-million dollars worth of video equipment in their clubhouses for the benefit of their players. Tony Gwynn was the guy who started all of that. In fact, in those days we didn't have the money to supply a video room. Tony Gwynn went out and bought the video equipment on his own. That was the start of all video programs being in major league baseball today.

Tying Tony to a **CONTRACT*** was another factor. He had a great agent, John Boggs. Very dedicated. A player's agent. He looked out for the player. Never looked out for himself. He was always trying to do something to help Tony Gwynn. He was a great guy to work with. He understood the game and he and Tony had a tremendous relationship.

The first time I met Tony Gwynn was when we drafted him. I was probably his biggest supporter at that time because I was the one that saw him the most. Of all the players I've ever scouted, I was more convinced that this guy was going to be more outstanding than any player I've ever drafted. He had some intangible that I can't describe. I just knew this guy was going to do it.

Once you get to know an employee and find out what kind of guy he is you can see that he was determined that he was going to be the best at his profession. He took no shortcuts. If it meant going out and buying video equipment on his own, then that's what he did. I can remember him having his wife

*After the Padres went to the 1984 World Series, Gwynn signed a new **CONTRACT** with the team for much less than the market level. Gene Orza, who was a high level executive with the baseball players union, screamed profanities at Gwynn when he first saw him after signing that contract.

tape all his games when he was on the road. He was a great guy to study the game. He probably could tell you the first pitch that anybody ever threw to him.

I wish all my players were like Tony Gwynn as far as attitude goes. All you needed to do with Tony Gwynn was wind him up and let him go to work. He took care of everything. He was probably the most prepared guy in the modern game. He didn't need a manager, he didn't need a coach, he didn't need anything. He knew what he had to do and he prepared himself well. There were no shortcuts with Tony. I used to love this guy. The way he came out to the bullpen about one o'clock every day. He hit every day. He hit every day! I would say that in the ten years I saw him take batting practice and watched him, I don't think he hit 10 balls out of the ballpark during batting practice. He was determined to keep the stroke, that core inside out stroke in between third and the rest of the line and shortstop. He had it down. He had it measured.

> All you needed to do with Tony Gwynn was wind him up and let him go to work.

To become a Gold Glove outfielder, he worked at it. He came out every day at one o'clock and hit for about an hour. And then, when we took regular batting practice, where was Tony Gwynn? He was out in right field, checking the walls, testing balls off the walls. Finding out where he was in the outfield.

After I left San Diego and managed elsewhere, our relationship was like father and son. "My man, my man," he used to call me. I got a card from him years ago and it says "Jack,"—he used to call me Trader Jack—"Thanks for all your help. You probably were the most important guy in my career."

Off the field, you never had to worry about Tony Gwynn getting into any trouble. After the game, up to the room and play some cards with Greg Booker and a few others. Those guys, I don't think they ever left the hotel after a game. Booker had Tony down in North Carolina to give clinics. They were very close. They played in Puerto Rico together. They and their wives are very close friends.

Here's what you see players do anymore. In the ninth inning, you're in a close game. You're down by a run. You're leading off the inning. You want the player to get on base, get hit by a pitch, or take a walk. What happens? They're swinging. Two and 0, they're swinging. Three and 0, they're swinging. Because they know they're going to get paid regardless. They think the more hits they get, the more they get their average up, the more they're going to get paid. You watch the game someday now. You watch two and 0, or three and one, the hitter is swinging. I watch the game every night and I see teams down 3-1 in the ninth inning and you're leading off the inning, you've got to get on. If you hit a home run, you're still down by one. That's the thing that bothers me, the selfishness.

That's why in 2003—and I'll say this on the record—I had the most unselfish team I ever had and managed in my career, the **FLORIDA MARLINS***. Those guys wanted to win so bad. They did all the little things and they never complained. They put the bunt on. Veteran players that played 10 years and 15 years in their careers they'd bunt. They didn't complain. They knew how to get the job done and they knew how to be unselfish. Just like Tony Gwynn did his whole career!

*The **MARLINS** are the only team that travels north to spring training... from Miami to Jupiter, Florida. The Marlins have never won their division, yet they have won two World Series.

SCOUT'S HONOR

BOB CLUCK

Bob Cluck grew up in San Diego and went to San Diego State. As a left-handed pitcher he owned the Aztecs strikeout record for 23 years and his college career ERA still ranks ninth in school history. Cluck found success as a coach and manager in the professional ranks with the Houston Astros, Oakland A's and Detroit Tigers. For 35 years he was the director and founder of the San Diego School of Baseball. He is the author of ten books on baseball.

I was on the coaching staff with the Houston Astros in '81 when Tony was drafted by San Diego State. The Astros did not have a pick in round one or two. Our first pick was going to be in the third round and we were all set up to take him.

I was disappointed when I saw the Padres draft him. But, you know, those things happen in the draft all the time. It was special for me because he was a kid I knew and he was playing for San Diego State. I am an alumnus there so that made it different. Many, many times you get burned in the draft.

Actually, it happened in Houston with Derek Jeter. In 1992, I believe it was, Hal Newhouser, our scout, had Jeter agree to sign for $600,000. We had the number one pick in the country. To a man, our scouting staff loved Jeter. Newhouser is from Michigan and played for the Tigers. Jeter's father was a big fan of Hal Newhouser. Minutes before the draft, our owner, John McMullen, walked in and said, "Caminetti's knees are shot. We need a third baseman. We're going to take Phil Nevin." Nevin was Cal State-Fullerton's third baseman and was College Player of the Year. You could've heard a pin drop. There were 25 scouts in there and we had Jeter on the board as the number one pick. So, we took Nevin because that's what the owner said. Newhouser quit. Gwynn and Jeter would have made nice teammates in Houston.

The reason I wanted to take Tony is that I was, and still am, adamant about athletic ability. It just seems that you really go long when you draft athletes. The only hang up about Tony was his arm. He had an extremely weak arm. He played in left field and couldn't throw at all. That's the only reason to me that he didn't go even higher. The other thing was that he really didn't have a lot of exposure to us in his senior year because he played basketball. He came out late and about the time he started to hit the season was over. In his senior year during the basketball season he was working out and hitting and he was much more prepared. Back then, the college baseball rules were such that alumni could come and help out. I had coached there some in the wintertime between seasons. I had seen Tony a lot so I had first-hand knowledge of what he was all about. Here was a guy who had been a point guard in basketball who was cool in arenas full of people. All the makeup stuff was A-plus—the kind of person he was, the work ethic, and if the problem was a weak arm, we could work on that. Which in fact he did and he actually had a pretty good arm when he reached the major leagues.

> I was the guy who made the call to bring Tony up to the big leagues.

I could never have imagined that he would work so hard that he would win five Gold Gloves. He had such a long way to go in order to learn the stuff—how to charge the ball and so on. We felt that although he had an average throwing arm he would play above average because of the way he charged the ball, his instincts, and his knowledge of the game. When you start making a projection from a poor arm to an arm that plays above average, you're really dreaming. It just doesn't happen that often. I mean he could always catch the ball, but throwing was such a minus. I don't know that he would have been drafted even that high if it hadn't been for Bobby Meacham. He was on the same team. Every scout was in to see Meacham and by accident they saw Gwynn and started to appreciate what he could do.

I had the last laugh. I was the guy who made the call to bring Tony up to the big leagues. I was in San Diego and Tony was in manager Doug Rader's office in Hawaii when I called. Doug handed him the phone and I said, "Tony, you're coming to San Diego." And he goes, "Great!" He was having a wonderful year and he came right in. Dick Williams saw him and liked him a lot, even though Williams didn't like young players very much.

Tony had great athletic ability, but the way his hands worked was incredible. The way he adjusted to pitches in different areas and at different speeds was impressive. I watched him for a long time very closely. Tony was a partner with Alan Trammell and me in our baseball school for 18 years. I watched him teach kids for 18 years. When he was at San Diego State the way his hands worked was the thing that sold me on him. That, and his prowess from basketball. He wasn't afraid of anything. Being on a baseball field did not make him nervous. He just had a lot of composure and a lot of polish from day one.

One reason Tony won batting titles was that he hit left-handers. I am a left-handed guy and when I was throwing to him he didn't budge. The old story is that until you tell a guy he's not supposed to hit left-handers, he'll hit them. Nobody ever told him, I guess, that he couldn't hit left-handers, so he did.

You know what's crazy about Gwynn's eight batting titles is that he should've won 10. I think he hit .358 one year and didn't win a batting title. Someone in Colorado hit .365 and Tony missed a batting title that should've been his. Those numbers in Denver were really inflated. A couple of those years he had great batting numbers but finished second because of the Colorado stuff.

I knew he was going to be something really special right away. It didn't take long to find out how good he was. I'd be lying if I told you I saw him at San Diego State and said, "There's a guy who's going to win eight batting titles." Nobody's crazy enough to think that at that point in time, but I would've told you he was going to be a hitter.

He joined us as one of the directors at the San Diego School of Baseball in his third year as a Padre and was with us for 18 years. I watched him at the end of six hour days sign autographs for an hour and a half, when everybody else was gone home. No kid ever left our baseball school without Tony Gwynn signing their glove or their hat, because he signed everybody's. No questions asked. He just said, "Line 'em up." He did that all over town. This was a guy who never said no to anybody. The only guys I ever saw do that throughout their careers were Alan Trammell, Luis Gonzalez, and Tony Gwynn.

After the strike year of 1995, we wanted to do something to reconnect with fans. We came up with the Padres Scholars idea, where we'd give middle school kids money to go to college. With all ideas like this, we went to Tony first. He was our barometer on community relations, and we wanted to get his reaction. He not only loved the idea, he wrote a five-figure check on the spot to show how much he supported the program. And then, he walked around the clubhouse and got other players to buy in.

—**Larry Lucchino**, Boston Red Sox president, former San Diego Padres president

A TOWERING FIGURE
WITH THE PADRES

KEVIN TOWERS

Kevin Towers was General Manager of the Padres in Tony Gwynn's final seasons. Towers was drafted by the Padres in 1982 after being the ace of the BYU staff. Until recently, he was GM of the Arizona Diamondbacks.

When I played in the Padres minor league system, I was an early riser...first one in the clubhouse in the morning. A lot of big-leaguers send their excess shoes over to the minor league side. One day I was there at 6 a.m. Sure enough the new shoe box was there in the clubhouse. I rummaged through looking for size-10. About the fourth set I looked at was a beautiful pair of brown kangaroo skin Nikes with number 19 on the back. I said "wow." I was a pitcher, not a hitter but I said if I'm wearing Tony Gwynn's shoes it can only be good.

I had to put a pitching toe on 'em. I never told Tony I got those shoes. I was just very excited to have them. They were the nicest pair. The softest and looked the best of the bunch. Just having the "19" on the back, I felt honored walking around the minor league clubhouse wearing shoes of the best player on the ball club.

When I first got the job as a GM in 1995, Tony really helped with my transition. Being an executive is tough after being a player. My last year playing was '89 so it was only six years between playing and running the entire organization. When I got the job, to be able to walk down to the clubhouse and have Number 19 walk up and hug you with a big smile, telling you how happy he was I got the job gave me instant "cred" within that clubhouse.

> He had respect for my position and he would always give me his honest opinion.

I was nervous being 35 years old and only being a scouting director two years, not even really having a lot of experience in the front office. Any trade I made, I usually ran it by Tony. He knew the good people and had access to people in other clubhouses. My first trade was when I traded Bip Roberts for Wally Joyner. I knew Wally well because I played with him at BYU. I just wanted Tony's reaction if I traded Bip and brought in Wally Joyner. He winked at me, put his thumb up, and I said, "enough said." That was the first trade I made and one of my better ones. Wally was part of our titles and the '98 World Series and really helped with the clubhouse chemistry, too.

Tony had respect for my position and he would always give me his honest opinion. I give him a lot of credit. The great thing about Tony is that he looked at players the way the GM does. It wasn't just the skill set, he understood the chemistry in the clubhouse and how important it was to put that puzzle together. He did his research and due diligence, making some calls to people he knew to find out what kind of guys they were. Having that kind of access in the clubhouse...you can't put a dollar sign on it.

I'm glad I didn't face him as a pitcher at BYU. I don't think the results would have been very good.

I remember the first time I saw him break out the Betacam on the next pitcher he was going to face. He was over looking at his last three or four games at bats against that pitcher. He wanted to be able to create an edge. If it was off-season conditioning programs, he'd be down there working out, trying to get himself in shape and ready for the start of every season. He had no vices, either. That was the beauty of Tony. It was baseball,

baseball, more baseball. If he wasn't on a baseball field, he was out in the community helping the youth of San Diego. He was a great role model. He was a baseball junkie.

I still drive a Ford truck because of Tony. He didn't do a whole lot of ads, but he was with Ford right up until the end. He used to do those commercials all the time. If a Ford is good enough for Tony Gwynn, it's good enough for Kevin Towers.

Dick Dent was our trainer at the time and a former Army Captain in Vietnam. Probably one of the toughest sonofaguns I've ever been around. His off-season conditioning programs were like Navy Seal camp. You showed up and you were going to be worn out by the end of the day. If you didn't put the work in Dick would tell you not to come. Dick was really, really good for Tony early in his career. Tony was banged up. His knees weren't all that good and Dick kept him on the field and you can't put a dollar sign on that one.

I don't think the weight impeded his game at all. I was just more worried about it would do to his lower half. The pounding in the outfield carrying extra weight was going to take its toll on his knees and it ultimately did. I remember walking into the clubhouse and seeing him draining I don't know how many CCs of fluid out of his knees right at the end of his career. I was sad. He had to get his knee drained twice a week just to be able to go out and play. I don't know if it had anything to do with his weight, but it didn't stop him from being a great hitter and a great defender. They always talked about the weight of Tony and Kruk. Both of them ended up being pretty darned good players.

My first year in pro ball was in Walla Walla, too, the year after Tony was there. A lot of sweet onions and a state penitentiary. The Past Time Café in Walla Walla...where all the players ate. Stayed at the Whitman College dorms, took a shower and by the end you were usually standing in two feet of water. Drain would get plugged up. You had to keep your windows shut because mosquitos would come in and bite you at night. After a ball game we'd all head over to the Past Time Café. It was one of those places where you put a quarter in and music would play at your booth. That was the spot.

With the Padres, Tony was as good a person as he was a player. We used to play cards. I loved playing cards with him. He was a terrible card player. When Tony got tired watching video in his room Wally Joyner and myself and Bruce Bochy would call him and invite him up to to either my suite or Bochy's suite for a game of Texas Hold 'Em. Not big stakes but usually Tony ended up leaving the room and he'd say, "Well, once again, boys you got my meal money."

He really wasn't a good poker player at all. I think he really just came up to laugh at the jokes and stories that we told and he figured it was worth the meal money to have a good time instead of sitting alone in his hotel room.

I played **GOLF*** with him a few times. He had a mad slice. He went off left-handed. He would play fairway to fairway. He would aim at the adjacent hole and end up in the middle of our fairway. He had that knack like he did hitting. I used to watch him set up cones in the outfield. He wanted to place a ball regardless of where it was thrown. Within 3 or 4 feet...bingo. I always said that he'd win most home run hitting contests if he wanted to. I wouldn't say he had huge power but he definitely had "over the fence power" and if he wanted to hit home runs, he could.

He could steal signs. He was a great base stealer. He claimed that right-field corner in Jack Murphy, which was a tough corner. You had to go up and underneath the bullpen bench to pick up ground balls. Even at the end of his career, not too many people would take an extra base on him. He'd always cut the ball off and it was always a perfect throw into second base.

---

*Only three people have ever appeared on Scotland's five-pound note: Queen Elizabeth II, the Queen Mum, and **JACK NICKLAUS**.

Only a handful of guys have ever stolen 5 bases in one game and Tony was one of those. On a scale of 20 to 80 he had 80 instincts for the game. There weren't many times that I can remember Tony Gwynn taking an extra base and getting thrown out when he shouldn't have. He knew the score, studied the scoreboard, knew situations and knew what he had to do when he was at the plate. Just very smart in the aspects of the game.

He would have made a good major league manager with his demeanor and communication skills...he knew the Xs and Os. The great managers are the ones who know how to communicate with players and that was pretty evident at San Diego State. Some managers now have a hard time understanding today's player. Not to say you have to agree with today's player or enable today's player but just understand them. It was evident at San Diego State that he was able to understand today's player. Most of this generation grew up with iPads and iPhones and Tony grew up with VHS and Betamax. No cell phone....

> Good dad, great role model, incredible hitter, incredible base runner, incredible fielder.

I dipped tobacco most of my life. I stopped five years ago. Off and on I'll do it, not much. Growing up in Oregon, my grand-dad was a logger and that's what they did. I started before I got into baseball because that's what loggers did up there.

I've heard it's worse than quitting heroin. Tony and I never talked about it after I quit. I would quit ...and the longest time was five years. It is tough when you're around baseball. It's so prevalent. I dipped the other day...the stress of my job. I'd rather throw in a dip of tobacco than have a drink.

Tony Gwynn was one of those dream players that come around once a century. In every aspect. Good dad, great role model, incredible hitter, incredible base runner, incredible fielder.

The word "Special" doesn't give justice to who he was.

BACK HOME AGAIN IN INDIANA

DALE RATERMANN

Dale Ratermann, author of 14 books, was the Senior Vice President of Market-ing for the **INDIANA PACERS**.* *Retired for almost a decade, he travels the world in search of crazy adventures and a lower golf handicap.*

In the mid '90s, our Director of Ticket Sales walked into my office one morning, and said, "Do you have a couple of tickets we can get for Tony Gwynn?" I said, "Tony Gwynn, the baseball player?" He said, "Yeah, that Tony Gwynn."

I said, "Which game does he want to come to?" The guy said, "Not a game. He wants to buy season tickets." And I said, "You're kidding me, right?" He said, "No, I got a call from him and he's interested in getting a couple of season tickets. Evi-dently he's going to be here all winter."

We came up with a couple of good seats for Tony once we found out that he definitely was moving to a suburb of Indianapolis and was going to spend the winter there. It turned out that his wife was involved in a couple of businesses that were located in the Indianapolis area and Tony had agreed to let her and her business interests take the forefront during the winter, in the off-season, while he took the forefront during the baseball season.

As a matter of fact he did come to practically every home Pacers game from November through the end of January, before he had to leave then, and head off to spring training. That continued for

*When UCLA coach Steve Alford was a senior in high school in 1983 in New Castle, Indiana, his high school team averaged more people in attendance per game than the **INDIANA PACERS**.

years. He sat in the second row right behind the Pacers bench. I met with the usher for that section and told him that if Tony ever had a problem with people bothering him, wanting to talk to him, wanting to get autographs, let us know. We'll make certain that he'll be able to sit and enjoy the game.

Every now and again, I'd check in with the usher. He'd tell me that nobody stops by, nobody knows who he is, nobody recognizes him. Later on we found out that Tony loved living here in the winter because it wasn't a baseball town. He loved the fact that he could go to the grocery store, and he could drive down the street, he could pop into the McDonald's or wherever, and come to a game, and nobody ever recognized him. Nobody ever bothered him for an autograph, and, not that he wouldn't have signed for the handful of people that did recognize him, but he just liked being a regular guy.

For that reason he kept coming back and coming back. Now, he made it known to us that anytime we wanted anything, to let us know. So, when we were getting our expansion WNBA team, we had to sell X number of tickets in advance. It was nine thousand tickets a year in advance of the start of our season. Most of the other teams that had preceded us, when they reached the milestone of 1,000 season tickets or 2,000 season tickets, would have some local dignitary actually make that purchase, so that the team could announce in a press release that "the mayor just bought in and he bought the thousandth season ticket." Our Senator at the time, who had actually crafted the legislation for Title IX which allowed women equal opportunities in the world of sports, bought our 2,000th ticket.

When we were approaching our 3,000th season ticket, it just so happened that that week Tony Gwynn got his **3,000TH CAREER HIT***. We came up with the idea that maybe we ought to have

*No hitter born in the 20th century with over **3,000 HITS** had a higher average than Gwynn. According to the Elias Sports Bureau, no hitter born since 1918—in other words, since Ted Williams —has even had 2,000 hits, and an average as high as .338.

Tony buy our 3,000th Indiana Fever ticket. We contacted him, and he said, "Yeah, by all means. Sure, where do I send the check?" Sure enough, he bought the 3,000th ticket for the Indiana Fever that enabled us to eventually get to the quota that we needed. Now, the Fever play all summer, so he never had a chance to see the team in person, but he was such a big basketball fan that he was more than willing to support us in any way he could.

We found out that 2002 was probably going to be the last winter that he was going to spend with us. We asked him if we could just have him do a hitting clinic, let us give him a little 'thank you' and present him with a jersey. He said, "By all means." If we wanted to do it, he was willing to go along with it.

He put on an absolutely unbelievable hitting clinic that hundreds of kids and parents and coaches attended. It was really, really really well received. He did a wonderful job, stuck around and signed autographs for everybody that was there. We had talked to him and asked, "How much do we owe you for this event?" He said, "Nothing, it's on me." We presented him with a jersey during a game and made it a Tony Gwynn Appreciation Night. He seemed to be pleased by it, and then when he went back to his seat after receiving that award, a lot of people around him were, "Wait a minute. That guy sitting there all these years, that's Tony Gwynn." It was a real surprise to people that he'd been sitting near by.

> The Gwynns were a total credit to the city of Indianapolis.

He was a huge basketball fan at all levels. I never asked him if he had concentrated on basketball if he would have been able to play at this level. As far as I know, he never wanted to ask if he could come and shoot around with the players. He just wanted to come and have something to do in the winter and enjoy the experience, enjoy being involved, and just enjoy watching the game.

I talked to him three or four times and he was really nice, really gracious. He always said, "If you guys need anything just let me know." He never had any requests to do anything out of the ordinary. It was only a handful of people who recognized him and went up to him and got his autograph during a game, up until that last game when he was with us in 2002 and then everyone knew who he was.

The Gwynns had a home in Fishers, Indiana, an Indianapolis suburb for at least 10 years. They had several businesses and a foundation here. They had Studio 815, which was a recording operation, and Tony's wife Alicia had a sportswear company called Steady Play, which was based in Fishers. They also had the Tony and Alicia Gwynn Foundation here.

They got involved in Indianapolis, through a pastor named John Key, who had a singing group called the New Life Community Choir. Alicia Gwynn had heard a CD of their singing and had brought the choir to San Diego to their church group there.

Marshall Faulk, the star running back for the Indianapolis Colts, was a San Diego State guy, which made Tony an instant Colts fan. With our Pacers, Reggie Miller was the big star, and Reggie had grown up near Tony's Long Beach home. In addition, Reggie's brother Darrell was a major-league baseball player. One time, the Colts asked Tony to speak to the team before they were leaving for an important game in Miami. The Colts were way behind at halftime, and Jim Harbaugh brought the Colts back in the second half to a win that had to make Gwynn very happy.

But the best thing the Gwynns did when they were here was that they bought and renovated a block of homes on the north side as a home for pregnant teens and as workplaces for the disadvantaged. The Gwynns were a total credit to the city of Indianapolis.

A HARD WAY TO MAKE AN EASY LIVING

TERRY KENNEDY

Terry Kennedy was drafted by the St. Louis Cardinals in the first round out of Florida State in the 1977 draft. He spent 14 years in the big leagues including six years with the San Diego Padres. Kennedy is now a scout for the Chicago Cubs. His father, Bob Kennedy, was a long time major league player, manager, and scout, and taught Ted Williams how to fly airplanes during the World War II.

Tony was very quiet in the beginning. The thing that stands out baseball-wise was that he wasn't a great outfielder when he came up. I wouldn't say he was a poor outfielder because that's not true. He was below average. He made himself into a Gold Glover with constant focus on the skills needed to throw somebody out. He made no excuses. He's the one that realized what needed to be done, and did it. That's just another example of his work ethic. He was born with tremendous hand-eye coordination but he made himself what he was through his work ethic, not only at the plate, but on the field and on the bases. He was a "plus" player everywhere, and it was because of how hard he worked and how much time he put into it. That was a great example for young players and veterans alike because it never changed, ever, throughout his career.

I wish I would've spent more time with him. He was usually with the younger players. He hung out with Kevin McReynolds and some of the other guys. It was my honor to be on his team because that's the way it was. He was the best player on our club and being in that lineup with him made all of us better— He would never claim that though.

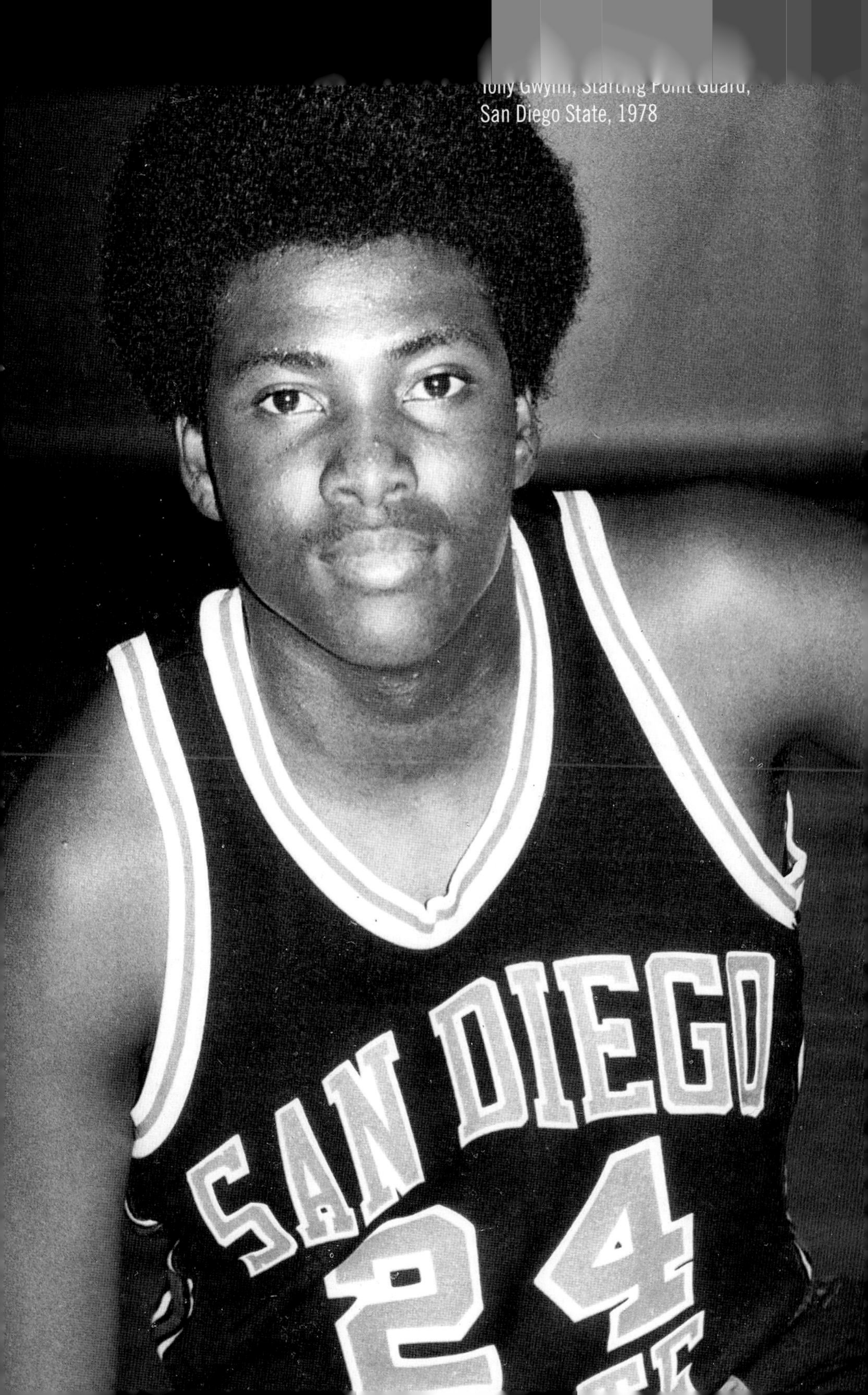

Tony Gwynn, Starting Point Guard,
San Diego State, 1978

Tony Gwynn (right) was drafted by the NBA Clippers the same day he was drafted by the Padres

Tony Gwynn with John Kruk, Spring Training in Yuma, 1986

1991—Trainer Bob Day checks out Gwynn's injured knee

February 1991. Tony Gwynn signs his contract. With him is his agent
John Boggs (L) and Padre GM Joe McIlvaine (R).

October 1989, Tony Gwynn serves coffee at McDonald's in Mira Mesa as part of McDonald's Founder's Day celebration.

January 1994, Tony Gwynn holds an informal meeting with reporters to discuss the two-year extension of his contract. Standing at the bar (l–r) Randy Smith, Padres General Manager, and John Boggs, Gwynn's agent.

Spring Training 1987

Tony Gwynn accepts 2012 Living Legend Award at Louisville Slugger Museum and Factory.

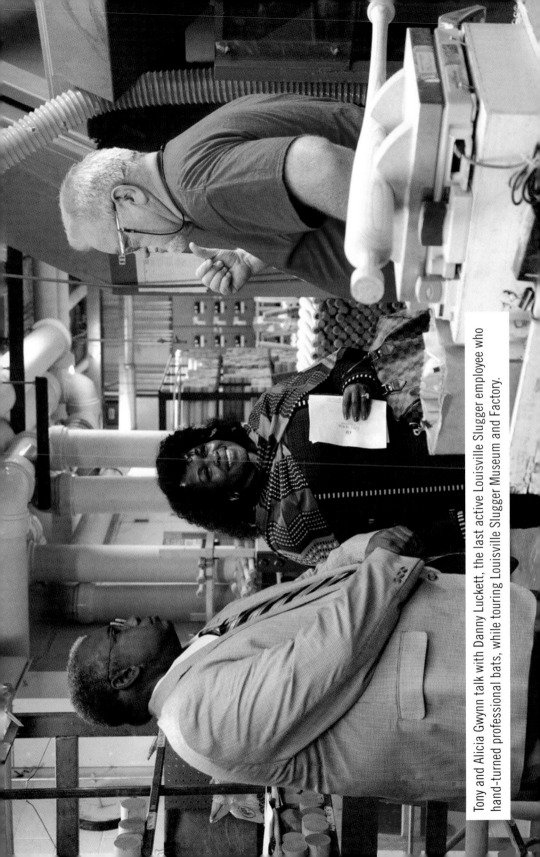

Tony and Alicia Gwynn talk with Danny Luckett, the last active Louisville Slugger employee who hand-turned professional bats, while touring Louisville Slugger Museum and Factory.

June 26, 2014, With pictures of Tony Gwynn on a monitor in the background, Clifford Esquibel, daughter-in-law Monica Esquibel, with 7-month-old son Carlo, and Monica's nephew Gabriel Mata, 11, lie on the grass near the Tony Gwynn statue before the start of the Tony Gwynn Memorial Tribute at Petco Park.

June 26, 2014. A number 19 was painted on the field at a memorial for Tony Gwynn at Petco Park.

Tony Gwynn talks to the crowd after being presented with a motorcycle.

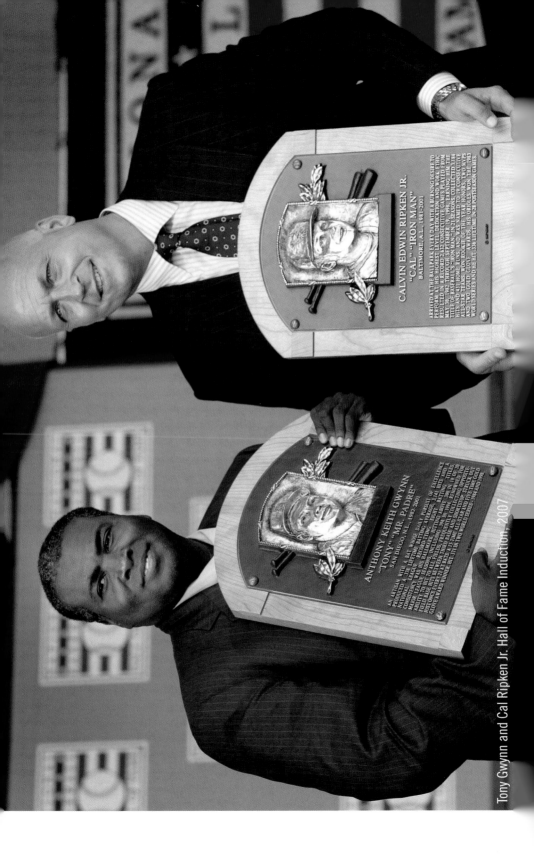

Tony Gwynn and Cal Ripken Jr. Hall of Fame Induction, 2007

Big West Coach of the Year

Retirement Ceremony Day. Photo by Jim Baird, not Norman Rockwell

Tony Gwynn chats with Chairman of the Board of Hillerich & Bradsby Co. (Louisville Slugger), Jack Hillerich at the 2012 Living Legend Award Ceremony

Cooperstown Induction Weekend, 2007

Cooperstown Induction Weekend, 2007

Tony Gwynn watching his life flash by on the scoreboard video screens.

June 26, 2014

Tony and Alicia Gwynn

Padres Lineup, Tony Gwynn's debut 1982

June 19, 2014, Workers hang a giant Tony Gwynn Padres jersey on the side of the San Diego County Administration Center to honor Gwynn, who died earlier in the week.

Cooperstown, 2007

ANTHONY KEITH GW
"TONY" "MR. PAD
SAN DIEGO N.L.

Gwynn just before his final game

Another long Tony Gwynn Drive, 2004

2007—Largest Cooperstown Crowd Ever

June 18, 2014, The scoreboard during a video tribute to former Tony Gwynn before the Padres game against the Mariners.

Donnie Walsh, Pacers President, makes Tony Gwynn an Honorary Pacer

Good-bye

He was a very quiet and reserved guy especially at the beginning when he was watching to see how things were done. He was the perfect rookie. There was nothing you had to tell him because he came to the park prepared. He knew he had to be prepared, too. That all came out of his personal ethic and also because of basketball and the high-quality competition he played against.

> **He was the perfect rookie.**

Tony won his first batting title in '84. Winning that title and then his continuing hitting right through the playoffs, coming up with the big hit, and having a good Series demonstrated to me that this guy was different. That he was going to be one of the all-timers. Nothing fazed him. Nobody on the mound fazed Tony. They came up with all kinds of statistics. Look at his stats against Maddux and Martinez—he didn't strike out against either of those guys in 125 at bats. He really emerged in that year of '84 with the batting title and the big hit in the fifth game of the playoffs against Cubs. It was a sign of things to come. None of us doubted that. We were already starting to rely on him....

I don't think Tony dipped tobacco more than any other guys. At that time there were still a lot of guys smoking. I'm sure the entire St. Louis team smoked when I was there. Throughout my career, many, many guys dipped. It's all a crapshoot. Some guys dipped their whole lives, and nothing happened, and other people this can happen. I know that Alicia wanted to get him to stop but it's just too bad. I still see young players still doing it and it's like they couldn't care less. I don't know what it is about baseball that you have to have something in your mouth—sunflower seeds, gum, something. You're always spitting. It's such a strange thing. I don't know what the psychology is behind that.

I was aware that Tony had been incommunicado for a few months. I was in San Diego in May for the 30th reunion of our

'84 World Series team. Garry Templeton told me that he had spoken to Tony a few months before. Garry told me that Tony was at home, that the family was very quiet about it, and the college had respected this. I asked Templeton if he thought Tony was going to make it and he said he didn't know. And then, sure enough, not even 10 days later it happened. To lose the two greatest people in the organization within one year—Jerry Coleman and Tony—it's a lot.

I was fortunate when I was younger. Something weird happened to me. I was in high school and I had some of that tobacco. It made me sick. I threw up for about three hours, and I never did it again. Thank goodness for that for me because I loved the smell of it. A lot of the guys would put Kahlúa in it and that made it even better. I loved the smell of it but I couldn't have it.

> He was joyful. That's what I remember. He was joyful playing the game.

Tony was a good family man. A real good family man. He loved his family. I know that he had a great relationship with his parents, and his brothers. He loved his kids. They were very proud of him and he was proud of them as a dad. He was a private person and his family was very important to him. In his role, people required a lot of things of him and he maintained that familial foundation. That was the basis for everything in his life. He never embarrassed his family, he never let them down, that's just the way he was. He was a great example to all of us—even the guys that were older.

He was joyful. That's what I remember. He was joyful playing the game.

THESE 7 THINGS ARE THE 10 REASONS TO LOVE TONY GWYNN

JERALD CLARK

Jerald Clark played for the San Diego Padres from 1988 until 1993, when he was traded to the Colorado Rockies. He became a longtime friend of Tony Gwynn on and off the field. Clark is a native of Crockett, Texas, and was drafted by the Padres in the 1985 draft.

Kurt Stillwell, Tony, and I were good friends. We went to spring training in Yuma one time and Tony decided to go to Bass Pro Shops and buy some lures, rods, and reels and the three of us would go fishing after a game. Well, Darren Jackson was on the team that spring and he joined in with us. One night, we worked on tying knots, fishing knots. I showed Tony how to do it so I wouldn't have to tie them all for him and he said, "Okay, okay I got this." We went out the next day after our workout. I told him to tie his first knot. He tied a knot, then he just pulled a random lure out of the box. He tied it on and cast it out there. He's throwing it out there and the thing just kept going and going. I said, "Tell me, how many knots did you tie?" He said, "I don't know, but it wasn't enough." He just threw away a six-dollar lure, so I told him just let me do it because I didn't want him to lose any more of his lures.

One time, when we were playing in Chicago, we went fishing on Lake Michigan and Tony caught a real big lake trout. Huge! Me, Tony, and Darren Jackson took a picture of it. He could beat you in about anything. I would go over to his house and play tennis and I couldn't beat him at tennis. I played basketball with him one time. At the time I didn't know of his accolades at San Diego State. He was shuffling the ball around and I said, "Hey Tony, you got a little touch." And he goes, "Well, back in my day I used to have a little something." I didn't realize until I got out of the game that he was an all-time assists leader at San Diego State in basketball. I told him, "Hey Tony, I don't understand. You can play everything. You can play basketball, you can play baseball, and you can beat me at **TENNIS***." He said, "Well, that's the way it is. But you can keep trying. Maybe you'll beat me someday, so just keep trying. But you're just not going to beat me."

When Tony got his 2,000th hit, I was excited but I had to contain my excitement. I had played with Tony for five years, we were good friends, we talked a lot, and we shared a lot of great things together. When he got his 2,000th hit, I was playing first base with Colorado. For some reason, I wasn't even thinking about it being his 2,000th hit. I thought it was just another hit until he ran past the bag and then came back. He looked at me, and I looked at him and I said, "Was that your 2,000th hit?" And he said "Yeah." I wanted to really congratulate him a whole lot more than I did, but I didn't want to show our pitcher up either. So I shook his hand and said, "Tony, that's a great job. I knew you could do it. Okay, now you've got 2,000 next you got to get to 3,000 because that'll get you into the Hall of Fame." And he said, "Yeah, I think I'm going to try to get that. I'm glad I'm here, man."

Tony was very special. He was just that kind of guy who went about his business every day. And he wasn't afraid of anybody. Some of us players who faced the tough pitchers and then the closer is coming in think, "Oh man, how am I going to get through this one?" I remember saying that to Tony one time, "I'm going up against this pitcher today. It's going to be tough

*In what sport was **CHRIS EVERT** the leading money winner in 1974? The answer: Horse racing. The owner, Carl Rosen, named his horses after tennis players. The horse named Chris Evert won $551,063 with five wins in eight starts.

because he's got a tough slider, he's a right-hander." Tony said, "Are you scared?" I said, "No, I'm not scared I'm just trying to figure him out." He said, "You just need to go up there and hit. You know how to hit so go out and hit. When he throws a strike you hit, that's all you need to do. There's nothing to worry about. I don't talk myself out of things. I go up there and do what I know I'm prepared to do. It's hitting the ball when it's in the strike zone. That's all it is."

Tony wasn't bashful but he wasn't boastful. He would tell you the truth. He would say what was on his mind. Some people didn't understand when Tony would say stuff like, "He's a really tough pitcher, but I got him tonight, and I will get him when I face him again." That was not boastful for Tony. He just looked at it as, "I did what I needed to do." He always had confidence in himself but he was not an arrogant guy. He downplayed himself but he also told you exactly what was going on.

> He'd say... "If you don't want to do it there're about 500 other guys in the minor leagues that will to do it."

He had a way about him and he was never tired. I never saw him come in and say, "I'm tired. My back is hurting. My knees are hurting." He would come in and say, "Okay, boys, strap it on." This was a guy who played 162 games a year and he would come in and say, "Strap it on."

For Tony, putting in the work and being prepared was his job. He'd say, "I have to entertain these people. These people come out to watch a baseball game. A lot of people are going to work every day. They have kids. They're not like making a lot of money. They're struggling. But, they're spending their hard earned money to come out and watch us entertain them. Don't shortchange these people by not running down balls, not hitting the cut-off man, and not giving 100%. These people want to be entertained so give them what they want. Go out and play hard and they'll keep coming out. If you don't want to do it there're about 500 other guys in the minor leagues that will."

He would take young players under his wing. He'd say, "Come on over here. I want to talk to you about something."

Tony was the same every day. He would never come in and be in a bad mood because somebody cut him off on the highway or somebody said something bad about him in the paper. Tony was the same every cotton-picking day and I don't know how he did it. He was just that way. All of us have bad games or losing streaks. Tony would say, "You know what. If you're losing now, today is the day you're going to turn it around. So, let's do it tonight." I'd struggle or sometimes I'd go 0 for 4, and I'd be trying to figure it out. Tony would say to me, "The game is over. If you want to correct that, come out tomorrow early. You can correct it, but the game is over now. Go home. Deal with it and then you can come back tomorrow and fix it." That was just the way he was.

Tony really loved his family. He loved his kids, he loved his wife, and he was a really good family man. Tony is a great example of what a man should do for his family. I know his wife and kids appreciated him and he would always talk about how great they were. He just got so much pleasure out of them. Tony really was a treasure.

Don Hansen of Temecula holds up a sign with a picture of him and Tony Gwynn, taken when Hansen was 8 years old, as his mother, Cathleen, wipes tears from her eyes near the end of the memorial to Tony Gwynn at Petco Park. Hansen brought the same sign with the picture to Gwynn's induction into the National Baseball Hall of Fame in Cooperstown in 2007.

Tony Gwynn acknowledges the Canadian crowd's applause after making his 3000th career hit at a game against the Expos.

Chapter Six

IT'S HARD TO CHEER WITH A BROKEN HEART

Fanecdotes

SO SAY YOU ONE, SO SAY YOU ALL

I remember him always wanting in on any prank or practical joke he could come up with, always asking bat boys to get him his "left-handed bat," or demanding the "keys to the batter's box" and sending kids on a wild-goose chase for them. Who was I to question Tony Gwynn as a 13-year-old? One day, he'd just taken money off of his teammates playing a card game called Casino. As they were getting up from the table, he asked me if I wanted to play. I told him I had work to get done before the game. So he told our clubhouse manager that I was indisposed, and then said he would play for only $20 a game. I only had something like $6 in my wallet, so he spotted me a $50 bill, and I pretty much thought I was the coolest kid around—14 years old, playing cards in an MLB clubhouse with Tony freaking Gwynn. I like to say I won $20 playing cards with him, which was my take-home, but given that he spotted me $50...

—**Tim Fischer**, Former San Francisco Giants bat boy, 1992–1996

I became a Padres fan in 1982, and I've never lived in San Diego. Tony Gwynn made me a fan. I used to go see the Padres play the Giants at **CANDLESTICK PARK**.* Being the only Padres fan in right field, I would call out to Tony, and he would always make eye contact, smile, and wave. The surrounding Giants fans would always give him respect and cheer for him, too. Even the opposing fans loved him.

—**Nathan Kiah Richards**, Fan, San Francisco

When I was 10, I was at a game super early at Jack Murphy Stadium watching batting practice. I remember all these kids, mainly older and mainly boys, were pushing and shoving to say hi to Tony as he walked by. They were all getting autographs,

*CANDLESTICK PARK** was the site of the last Beatles concert in 1966.

and I kept getting pushed back further and further. He pulled out a ball from his glove, signed it, and said, "Nope, this is for the little lady," and handed it to me. Made my day, plus I felt super cool in front of all those older boys.

—**Jessica Settle Cunningham**, Fan

When Tony Jr. was in high school, Tony Sr. arranged for school-colored Nikes for each of the boy and girl basketball players, all levels. And he pulled up in his SUV and delivered them himself. No fanfare. Just handing out shoes to the kids. At least he can hit some in heaven, and Jerry Coleman can Hang a Star on them over and over.

—**Chrisanna Weech Johnson**, Fan

I was a fan of the Padres long time before I was a player. My first trip to San Diego Stadium came in 1978 when I was a freshman basketball player at San Diego State. As a youth in Long Beach, I grew up a Dodgers fan... Willie Davis was my hero.

But shortly after coming to San Diego State, I started paying attention to the Padres, and in 1978 a group of friends and I shelled out fifty cents apiece to go sit in the bleachers and watch the Padres play the Cubs.

Those were great times. We'd buy the cheapest bleacher seats and start working our way forward through the stands. We'd make a game of seeing how long it would take us before we'd be sitting in the best seats behind home plate.

I remember going to see the Pirates play the Padres in 1979. I love the way the Pirates attacked the ball. We snuck all the way around to seats right behind the Padres dugout when Willie Stargell came up late in the game. We were so close that we could hear the Pirates talking in their dugout. Then Stargell hit this ball to right center... The swing, the contact, the sound, and the sight of that ball taking off. We were in awe. And we could hear the Pirates congratulating Stargell when he returned to the dugout. Pops! To experience major league baseball live. It was the greatest.

When I first arrived in San Diego, I usually went to San

Diego Stadium to see the other teams. But I saw the Padres so many times that I started to convert. They became my team. Like the Chargers and Clippers became my teams. I was a San Diegan. Soon I began tracking the Padres. Dave Winfield. Randy Jones. Ozzie Smith. I was supposed to be there the day Smith made that great bare-handed stop on Jeff Burroughs, but I stayed home and saw it on television... I kicked myself for missing that one.

You knew back then that you become a Padres fan when you started looking at the paper each day to see how close they were to .500. That was always the key deal. You didn't think about them winning a title back then, but if they were .500, that was an achievement. I remember 1978, when the Padres did have a winning record for the first time. That was huge.

Back then, I didn't think much about ever playing for the Padres. I was playing basketball at San Diego State. Even when I started playing baseball for the Aztecs, I didn't think much about playing for the Padres.

Then, in 1981, I was offered a chance to be an extra in a Padres commercial they were filming at the stadium. I put on a Padres uniform for the first time. Number 15. I had my back to the camera in the commercial, but I was a Padre that day. Four months later the Padres drafted me. I remember trying on the uniform again. It felt good. It just felt like that's where I belonged

Then there was that early morning in 1998 when our bus driver got lost taking us to a hotel in Montréal. We had been driving in circles for what seemed like hours when Kevin Brown spotted this kid walking along the road. Brownie ordered the driver to stop, and we got this kid on the bus to direct us to our hotel. It turned out that it was about three blocks away. But as we got off the bus, every one of the players tipped that kid— $20, $50, whatever we had. I remember that kid standing by the bus and looking at that wad of bills. I always wondered how he explained all that money when he got home.

—**Tony Gwynn** quoted by Bill Center in the
book *Padres Essential*

I was working for Cox Communications in 2009 as the VP/ General Manager overseeing the Padres telecasts. I'd occasionally bring my children to ballgames. During this particular game, my son, Connor, was with me in the broadcast booth, visiting with Tony and Mark Grant. Tony started asking my son all about his Little League games. He wanted to see Connor's batting stance, and gave him pointers. Connor was over the moon. As their conversation was concluding, Tony reached into a small bag he had beside his chair and pulled out a pair of worn batting gloves, saying, "These are mine and I want you to use them." The gloves were way too large for Connor's hands. He's kept them in a special pocket in his baseball bag all this time, though. This year was the first season when the gloves actually fit. He wore them every time he batted.

—**Craig Nichols,** Principal, The Kitchen Agency, San Diego

When I worked for the Padres, I had interviewed for a job with another team. I took the call in an office right next to where Tony would sit as he signed the items sent to him and read fan mail. He came in to do that. Well, I opened the door and squealed, "I got the job!" I felt bad that I interrupted him, apologized, and turned away to leave him to it. But he asked me about the job, what I would be doing, and everything else a person with genuine interest would ask. Then he stood, stuck out his hand, wished me well, and said the other team was lucky to get me. That is just a small fraction, of a small fraction of the wonderful person that he was. He really did care about the people he met. The man was so much more than just a ball player and his death has left a hole in this town and in the world.

—**Ramie Zomisky**, Former Padres employee

In high school, I wore number 19 to honor him. One game, he came to watch Adam Jones play, trying to recruit him to come to college instead of signing. I pitched that day and Coach liked what he saw. Because of him seeing me that day I got to go to SDSU with a scholarship, the only place I wanted to go. One day, I wanted to get my Pops something nice for his birthday,

I didn't have the money and I asked Coach if he could get me in contact with Oakley and get a discount on some sunglasses. He just took the sunglasses off his cap, cleaned them, and gave them to me, saying "Here, give these to your Pops." Coach believed in me. He told me he knew I'd make it. That I had what it takes. I don't think he understood how much that meant to me. But I did make sure he knew I loved and respected him, giving him a hug whenever I saw him. Loyalty is something I consider so important in a person's character, and one part of Coach that will live forever in the many people he mentored throughout his shortened life.

—**Bruce Billings**, Pitcher, New York Yankees

I used to work for the Jumbotron team by running the cord for the camera guy. This was in 1996. We had to get to the stadium really early to set up. I was eating in the press box and heard this crack of a bat coming from the field. I looked down and it was Tony Gwynn hitting ball after ball after ball from a batting tee. I remember thinking that was what little tee-ballers did, not the greatest hitter I'd ever known. Many years later, I was working in the ballpark press box as a writer. Tony's son had just been traded to the Padres. I looked down on the field, and again, the only ones down there way before game time working on fundamentals were Tony and his son.

—**Dan McLellan**, Former sportswriter

I would have been run out of town if I ever even thought of trading number 19! He was as close to being untouchable as any Padre I ever had. The negotiations with Tony were different than others. He NEVER wanted to leave this city or organization, and he always rolled his contract additional years before he entered his last year for that reason. He took significantly less to remain in SD because he loved it here. Tony was often my sounding board before I made a trade. Who better than Tony to either validate a deal or squash it? I had that type of confidence in his evaluation skills, and knew that he would know if a particular player's character would fit well in our clubhouse. Also, I loved to play poker with Tony on road trips. By winning, it allowed me to eat like a big leaguer on the road!

—**Kevin Towers**, Former Arizona Diamondbacks general manager; former Padres general manager, 1995–2009

He was our colleague and friend and he was family. But we called him Coach Gwynn-The teacher. He understood being a student-athlete was challenging. But he taught his core value: Do it right. He taught players to respect the game, to respect people, and to do it with class.

—**Mark Martinez**, Baseball coach, San Diego State University

I remember the first time I met him at an autograph signing. I was speechless as he talked to me and called me by name. One year later, I took my son to meet him and get an autograph. My son had the same response meeting his hero. Tony remembered me from the previous year. We were both dumbfounded. The look of awe and love on my son's face was priceless and a shared memory we will never forget.

—**Teresa Swift**, Fan

I remember paying an ungodly amount of money, at least for a college kid, for field seats to Tony's last game in 2001. After I bought the tickets, 9/11 happened and MLB pushed back the schedule, so I had to buy a second set of tickets to see Tony's last game, which also ended up being the game Rickey Henderson got his 3,000th hit. Tony, Jerry Coleman, and Junior Seau were really big parts of growing up in San Diego in the '80s and '90s. He's a legend.

—**John McCauley**, Fan

The single moment when I was most impressed with Tony Gwynn was right near the end of his career. It was hotter than blazes. It's early afternoon at Qualcomm Stadium. There's nobody around and there's only one player taking batting practice. It was 20 years after Tony broke in and he was still taking extra hitting. Who else would do that? That's why he was so successful.

Over the years, Tony Gwynn was beaten up and broken down. He was in such pain for many years, especially when it came time to travel. Flying killed his knee because of the altitude. One time near the end of his career, we were flying back from Pittsburgh. Tony was there in his suit, wrapped in a blanket, laying on the floor of the plane to straighten his knees, and ease the pain. People didn't see that part. They didn't see the wear and tear of travel, and having to come off the plane and be Tony Gwynn.

—**Tim Flannery**, former Padre teammate

In 1982, I told my pitching coach Tommy House, "Take this kid Gwynn out to Field 2, and show him how to grip a baseball, and how to throw it correctly." When he was throwing from the outfield, he couldn't throw it on a straight line to second base. He would throw arcing rainbows. Then we would have coach Rob Picciolo grab a bag of balls and hit him fly ball after fly ball, and hit him ground balls. Pretty soon he was an adequate fielder, and later he became a great fielder. The most treasured piece of memorabilia that Tony Gwynn said he owned was his first Gold Glove in 1986.

—**Dick Williams**, ex-Padres manager

Tony Gwynn would have had nine batting titles if not for me. Tony was the one who showed me that I could hit for average as well as power. He showed me how to do it. When I was traded from the Brewers to the Padres in '92 I had never batted better than .294. I almost won the Triple Crown and I led the league in batting at .330 thanks to Tony Gwynn.

—**Gary Sheffield**

I was volunteering at a district Babe Ruth tournament years ago. These thirteen- and fourteen-year-old boys playing their summer baseball. The district tournament was at Borleske Stadium in Walla Walla, WA.

I'll never forget this one kid who was not from Walla Walla. He was from out of town, but obviously he knew something about baseball, because he was standing at Borleske Stadium. As he was walking away after striking out, he said, "I just stood in the same batter's box that Tony Gwynn stood in." And that's all he could think about. That's probably why he struck out.

There are some other famous people who played baseball at Walla Walla. One was Ozzie Smith with the Padres. Kurt Russell, the actor, played in Walla Walla. He was a very good player.

—**Stephanie Mayer**, Walla Walla, Washington

Tony and I knew each other through the instruction leagues and spring training. As he went up through the ranks I was always a league behind him. He was in Amarillo when I was in Reno, and then I went to Beaumont, Texas. Amarillo became the Beaumont Golden Gators. Tony was in Hawaii by that time, and quickly made it to the big leagues. We just saw each other in spring training. Fortunately, he and I had the same shoe size, so he was always very nice to me when he left spring training. He always made sure that the guys who had his foot size had plenty of shoes.

In the minor leagues you find that mentally you almost want other guys to do poorly so you can do well. But you never wished that on Tony. Tony was just such a good guy. I was playing in Beaumont, and he was playing in the Astrodome. I got there early and he came out. He'd call me Leo, and he said, "Hey Leo, how are you doing?" Some of those guys get to the big leagues and don't have time for guys they'd gotten to know through the minor leagues. He just wasn't that way.

I went to an event where he was getting a lifetime achievement award from Louisville Slugger. As he was walking into the event, there were all kinds of people trying to hound him for an autograph. I was there with my son and my wife. I hadn't seen the man in twenty years. As he went by I said, "Hey Tony." He looked over and he said, "Hey Leo." He had a little entourage with him. He stopped security, came over and shook my hand, and asked how I was doing. But for him to stop when he's on his way to get an award to say hello to me—that was just Tony Gwynn. Even to remember my name after twenty years is amazing....

He was dipping all the time when I knew him. When we were in the **MINOR LEAGUES***, everyone just did it, tobacco was just the thing to do. I chewed tobacco. I never really dipped, like he did. Dip is the stuff you put in the front part of your lip, and chew is what comes out of the pouch and you chew on the side of your face. Red Man is chew and Copenhagen and Skoal are dip.

Nobody really ever talked about not using. I have a print from when I played at the University of Kentucky. It has a bat, a helmet, a glove and the players. There is a big logo of a pack of Red Man on the poster. It was part of the game then. They can talk about the dangers of it, but all through the Minor Leagues, and especially when you got in a Big League team situation, it was just there, rolls of Skoal and Copenhagen. It didn't become vogue to talk about its dangers until recently.

I've discouraged my son from doing it. There're kids who still do it now, even though it's not allowed on the field. Hopefully it changes. Actually, I know folks who have dipped all their life and never got cancer. I'm sure there's a correlation, but if it would help kids that don't ever chew because of that story coming out....But, they haven't really put out a whole bunch about Tony dipping. They've mentioned it, and he has actually talked about how it was a contributing factor to his cancer, but they've talked more about the kind of person he was, how good he was.

—**Jim Leopold**, Dayton native who was an outstanding baseball player at the University of Kentucky and was drafted in 1981 by the San Diego Padres, the same year that Tony Gwynn was drafted by the Padres. He is now an executive in the home office of Papa John's in Louisville, Kentucky

*When Hank Aaron was director of **MINOR LEAGUE** Operations for the Atlanta Braves in the early 90s, he had the pockets of the players' uniforms cut off so they couldn't carry tobacco.

I am the son of a Navy captain who commanded a squadron whose flagship was in Boston for repairs in 1959. My dad's boyhood pal was Mike Higgins, manager of the Red Sox. Higgins asked my dad if I would like to be the batboy. I was thrilled because Ted Williams was my absolute idol.

I got to know Ted Williams very well. I shined his shoes, oiled his glove, tarred his bat. I learned what a caring human being he was to "little people," regardless of how the press treated him.

Forward to 1992. I am living in San Diego and we receive an invitation to attend the ribbon-cutting for the Ted Williams Freeway. My wife and I are in the receiving line—I am now 48 years old and have not seen Ted since I was 15—and he approaches me, puts his hand on my shoulder, and says, "Hi Skipper, (the nickname he gave to me), it's been a long time."

Forward to 2002. Tony Gwynn is the baseball coach at SDSU and, as a board member of the Aztec Athletic Foundation, my wife and I develop a wonderful friendship with Tony.

Among thousands of examples I can give you of the man he was, one stands out.

I invited Tony to speak before my financial planners association at our holiday meeting. There were more than 400 people, most of whom had brought something for Tony to sign.

As emcee, I was shocked. No way was I going to allow Tony's time to be abused in this way. When I mentioned this to Tony, all he said was, "Larry, please don't stress."

That true gentleman stayed for over three hours, signed every item, and allowed everyone who had a camera to take a picture with him.

—**Larry Cook**, San Diego

Around 1995, I recall my co-worker, who was about eight months pregnant, gushing that Tony Gwynn had pumped her gasoline for her because she was so pregnant. What a kind gentleman.

—**Ellyn Quiggle**, La Jolla

I don't know how much money Tony had left when he died, but here's something nobody ever knew. They needed a new scoreboard for the Aztecs stadium, and Tony asked me If I could give him some of his deferred contract money to build it.

I think it was going to cost $100,000. It was a sacrifice for the Gwynns. But that was Tony. He loved the place. In many ways, college ball has the best group of kids, relatively anonymous, and most of them go away and do something else. Nothing wrong with that. And Tony loved it.

There is incomplete business to this. There are too many things I still wanted to ask Tony. I regret that. I know people who work hard, a lot of them. But I've never known anybody who worked harder than Tony Gwynn.

He was a really decent guy and I became drawn to him from the very beginning.

The first guy I called when I bought the team in December of '94 was Tony. He was easily my favorite on the club. I don't think he was particularly fond of that notion, but he didn't get a vote.

Tony will be remembered for his amazing work ethic. He worked harder than anybody, and it explained a lot.

I also became a big fan of Aztecs basketball and along the way noticed Tony, despite SDSU's recent success in the sport, held the school's career assists record (still does).

I asked him: "How, after all these years, can you still hold the school's assists record?" He answered, "Poor recruiting." We know that hasn't been the case. He was a great athlete. Tony was a strong man.

And focused. I've never seen anyone so focused. He was never out of a game. Maybe if he'd weighed 40, 50 pounds less, his wheels wouldn't have gone on him. But maybe when you're so focused on one thing, you have to give up something else, and in that non-sporting part of his life, he let things go.

—**John Moores**, Padres owner, 1994-2012

When I was a student at the University of Portland, I worked in the mail room of Nike during the summers. One day, one of my jobs was to process an order for Tony Gwynn, who was on the Nike staff. After putting the order together, I slipped a note inside saying, "Dear Tony, I just want you to know that there's someone in the Pacific Northwest who not only enjoys watching you play baseball, but respects the way you conduct yourself off the field." I signed my name to the note. I just always liked Tony Gwynn so I thought that would be a nice touch.

Three weeks later, I was opening all the mail as I did every day. There was a long rectangular box addressed to me of all people. I opened it up, and inside was an autographed bat from Tony Gwynn. I couldn't believe it, and to this day in my office in Miami I have that to remind me to conduct my affairs like Tony Gwynn did.

—**Erik SPOELSTRA**,* head coach of the NBA's Miami Heat

I never got to meet Tony Gwynn, but I did talk to him on the phone once. It was for a story I wrote about the idiosyncrasies of the strike zone, and I was thrilled to have gotten him on the line.

Imagine having the chance to talk to the greatest hitter since Ted Williams about his craft. Now imagine your phone dropping his call three times in a row.

It was a little more horrifying every time, and yet Gwynn would keep calling back some kid he'd never spoken with before in his life, laughing every time I answered.

Everyone seemed to have a connection with this man. A signed jersey, an encounter at a restaurant, a conversation at the mall—it didn't matter if you were a fellow Hall of Famer or a cashier at Vons. The king of San Diego always made you feel like royalty.

San Diego is full of people who came from somewhere else. But they all know Tony.

*Baseball Chapel was started in the 1960s by Detroit sportswriter Watson **SPOELSTRA** as thanksgiving for his daughter surviving a near-death situation. His grandson Erik, an Asian-American, is head coach of the Miami Heat.

And regardless of how long they've been here, they know this place will never be the same.

—**Matt Caulkins**, sportswriter

Tony Gwynn was a selfish player, but in a great way. In 1991, Tony Gwynn had the batting title in the bag at .342, but insisted on playing the last month with a bad knee, before having knee surgery on September 18. His average fell from .342 to .317, and Terry Pendleton from the Atlanta Braves won the silver bat with .319. In a game in 1998, when John Smoltz was pitching for the Braves, Gwynn had what I thought was the game of his life. Tony had skipped batting practice, and had a horrible knee and a bad heel. He went 0 for 4, but it was the greatest 0 for 4 I've ever seen. He put the ball in play every time. It was just incredible considering the condition his knees were in.

But the fields at Three Rivers in Pittsburgh, the Vet in Philadelphia, and Riverfront in Cincinnati were like cement, and they caused his left knee to swell way up. We drained gallons of liquid from the cartilage with huge needles. His left knee had eight surgeries, and at the very end of his career his right knee needed surgery too.

He saw the ball differently than anybody else. He saw things no one else saw. If the pitcher threw a change up, he could tell from the dugout. He sees the guy's fingers on the ball, and he knows. No one else sees the ball like that. It's not normal, you know. It's just not normal.

When he used to **STRIKE OUT*** swinging, the pitcher was shocked, shocked. Everybody in the stadium was shocked. He is the best hitter I've seen in all my years in the game.

*Gwynn had six straight seasons in which he **STRUCK OUT** fewer than 20 times. The day he announced his retirement, there were 29 players in the big leagues who had struck out more than 20 times that month. When he retired with a career batting average of .338, he could have played the next few seasons, had 1,200 at-bats without a hit, and still would've hit .300 for his career.

Tony would've hit .400 in 1994, I feel. It was the one year where he made it to the last month healthy. It was a shame, because he never focused on the numbers. All he thought about was the swing. Personally, I thought he lost three hits because of bad scorekeeping. Those three hits would've given him a .400 average.

Everything you hear about Tony is the swing, the talent, the smile. What people don't understand is how tough he was. He won batting titles when you didn't think he could walk down the ramp to the field. He played hurt better than anyone in the game.
      —**Merv Rettenmund**, former Padres hitting coach

I was an intern for a San Diego newspaper, when I approached Gwynn for my first interview. I was a nobody, yet he invited me to sit down and talk. I was thinking, "Wow, all baseball players are going to be like Tony Gwynn." If only that was true today.
      —**George Dohrmann**, later a *Sports Illustrated* writer.

Casa de Amparo is an organization that treats and prevents child abuse and neglect. The organization actually houses children who have been removed from their homes due to abuse and neglect, and we provide them with everything that they need while they are here with us. Tony Gwynn got involved with us through his foundation. We were the beneficiary of a golf tournament and a casino night fundraiser that he did for us.

Specifically, through his foundation Tony was very committed to helping our kids with their education. Sending them to school is not a main priority for their parents. That's one of the reasons they end up with us. Tony was very committed to their education, and he wanted a specific gift to go to pay the salary for a reading tutor. This reading tutor was extremely important because most of our kids were behind at least one to two grade levels.

Back then, there were two little girls who were sisters. An eight and a nine-year-old. They were three years behind in school, particularly with reading. They didn't have any confidence to read or to want to read, and by the time they left

Casa de Amparo in the six-month time that they were with us, they were brought up two reading levels due to being able to work with this reading teacher that Tony provided the funding. Obviously, what he did for our kids was extremely impactful.

—**Kathy Karpé**, Executive Director,
Casa de Amparo, San Marcos

I talked to George Brett before I went to Cooperstown just to get the lay of the land. He said, "It'll be four of the most unforgettable days of your life, and it'll be four of the fastest days of your life. There's a lot going on, and it goes by pretty quickly, so see if you can just slow it down and soak in every moment of it."

I didn't talk to Tony Gwynn before the ceremony. But he sat right next to me on the stage. It was a pretty hot and humid day, and we were all in coat and tie.

When we were backstage, getting ready to go up on the stage, they handed everybody a nice bottle of ice water. I set it down by the chair next to me. Tony and I were just chatting away. He started sweating bullets. Every once in a while, I would lean down and pick up the bottle of water, take a swig, and put it back down. I noticed after a couple of times that he kept staring. I didn't say anything. After I did that three or four times, he said, "Where did you get that water?"

> ...he grabbed me, and put his arm around my shoulder, and he said, "You may have saved my life."

I said, "Well, they gave us each a bottle when we came up on stage." He said, "Oh no! They must have missed me, or I must have missed them." I didn't know what to say to that. A couple of minutes later when I took a drink, he kept looking at it. So I said, "Hey, buddy, do you want to share this?"

He said, "Aaah, that would be great." He took the bottle, took a big drink out of it, and handed it back to me. I put the cap back on it, and set it back down. He said, "Aaah man, that was great!"

Then, when the inductions were done, we stood up and as we were walking off the stage, he grabbed me, and put his arm around my shoulder, and he said, "You may have saved my life."

We were up there laughing about it. I said "Thanks Tony. I'm glad I could have been a part of that moment for you." I don't know what happened, how come he didn't get his bottle of ice water, but I guess I saved him, at least for a few more years.

Later, we were talking about bats. He said he had one of his best years when he went through the entire season with the same bat. He didn't break or crack a bat for one whole year. He said, "I loved that bat."

I said, "I guess so."

He told me what he did that year and a couple of his stats. He said, "You know, I took that bat home with me at the end of the season, and then I took it to Spring Training. Wouldn't you know it, we were having batting practice the first day before we could play an exhibition game and I broke the darn bat." He said, "Just taking a batting practice! I was crying. I couldn't believe I broke that darn bat."

—**Denny Mathews**, inducted into the Hall of Fame the same day as Tony Gwynn. Mathews is the only play-by-play announcer the Kansas City Royals have ever had since their inception in 1969.

Tony and I are sitting in front of his cubicle at Qualcomm, and he's thinking about a couple of nicknames he had just read in history. He asked me what my favorite nicknames were, and I give him a couple that I really liked from the past.

He turns to Rickey Henderson and says, "Rickey, what's your all-time favorite baseball nickname?"

Rickey looks up at him and he goes, "Rickey."

Well, Tony laughed so hard he fell backwards on his stool and bumped his head, and it was that laugh that we all remember with Tony. And that laugh, there was nothing fake to it. That laugh came from his soul.

Everybody who's been in a Major League clubhouse knows how the clubhouse guys come around and they pick up the shoes, they shine the players shoes, and stuff. Tony Gwynn, throughout his career, always shined his own shoes. He never gave them to the clubhouse kids.

Early in his career, he talked about how his dad, Charles, visited him in the clubhouse, and Charles saw the clubhouse guys picking up the shoes of the players. And he said "What's that all about?" Tony said, "Ah, they shine the shoes for us." His dad said, "No, you shine your own shoes. They're your shoes, you shine them."

He looked at his dad and sort of smiled and said "This isn't funny" and Tony said from that point forward he made a habit of always doing his own shoes.

He's in Chicago and the Cub fans were always all over him. He's out there one day in right field, and the sun was a little bright, so he's got these wraparound sun glasses. He says every once in a while in a baseball game you can hear a fan who's on you. All of a sudden he hears this voice and it goes, "Hey Gwynn, I've got it. You're one of those Ninja Turtles. You got the big behind. You got the big stomach. And you got that funny looking thing on your face." And Tony said he's leaning over and he's trying hard not to laugh, but he's looking out the corner of his eye, and he can see the guy. He can see the guy along the low rail at Wrigley Field. So he says, "The inning ends, and I just make a beeline for the guy. I'm running as fast as I can towards this guy. The guy sees me coming, and security sees it, and they're coming down from both sides, and down out of the stands, 'cause they think there's going to be a confrontation."

> Tony loved being ribbed as much as he loved laughing and ribbing other people.

He says, "I get to that low rail and I reach out my hand, and I go, 'Hey, that's one of the best ones ever.' I shake his hand, and I take off running for the dugout. I wanted to turn around, look at the guy and see what the reaction was, but I knew that if I looked back it would ruin everything, so I just kept running."

He always was wondering what happened to that guy, and it was one of his favorite memories. I always loved that about Tony. He could take things that weren't the five-hit games, that weren't the four-for-fives, and he could remember all the small things.

There's a story in the Salt Lake newspaper, about how **DANNY AINGE*** was the greatest two-sport letterman ever to come out of the Western Athletic Conference. Tony saw it, and he was just like "What!" And he would laugh about it.

Well, I sent away and I got five copies of that paper and about once a week or once a home-stand, I'd roll one of those things up and I'd stick it in his mailbox. He'd look at it and he'd go, "Where'd this come from?" He'd start laughing, and he knew who was doing it. We had a lot of fun with that. But that's the thing, Tony loved being ribbed as much as he loved laughing and ribbing other people.

I'd like to say, "Hey, I remember this game when he got five hits." I don't remember that as much as just being with this truly unique and wonderful human being.

—**Bill Center**, long-time *Union-Tribune* writer

***DANNY AINGE** was the tallest second baseman in major league history. Ainge hit .220 with the Toronto Blue Jays 1979-81.

IF A BAT COULD TALK,
IT WOULD SOUND LIKE TONY GWYNN

GREG MADDUX

Greg Maddux made his major league debut as a pinch run-ner...an inauspicious start for the winningest living pitcher (355 wins). Maddux is a consultant for the Texas Rangers. He lives in Las Vegas.

It's a pleasure to talk about Tony Gwynn, although there have been many times in my career that I would not have said such a thing. With almost 800 major league games I have exactly one save. That save came against the Padres in the 1998 playoffs. I could not have had a worse batter to pitch to. Tony Gwynn owned me during his career. He hit .462 lifetime and I never struck him out in almost 90 at-bats. In fact, Pedro Martinez faced him about 35 times and never struck him out.

Anyway, they called me in for my only save opportunity and I was lucky enough to get Tony to ground out to second base and save the game for us. I actually thought I had struck him out on the previous pitch but I didn't get the call.

The word around the league at one time was that I was tipping my pitches to Tony. I would ask him about it and he would laugh it off. But after we both retired, I found out that I was tipping my pitches. Tony's eyesight and concentration were so good and his studying video was so persistent, that he saw that when I threw a changeup, the knuckle on my middle finger came up about a half inch higher than it did my other pitches. Hard to believe, but it's true.

For several years, Tony would come to a Las Vegas baseball camp that we had for kids in the off season. He was great with the kids, and when he saw a kid was struggling, he would take him over to the side and work with him one-on-one. You could not have had a finer instructor for young people. He just loved baseball. He was the greatest ambassador baseball ever had.

Another thing that really helped Tony was that he was a strong family man, and had a strong family foundation behind him. When I was inducted into the Baseball Hall of Fame with Joe Torre, Bobby Cox, Frank Thomas, Tony La Russa, and my teammate Tom Glavine, it was a great occasion. A fan at Cooperstown mentioned to me that I was the only one out of the six that had not gone through a divorce. That's a real tribute to my wife and it's a tribute to Tony's wife that they put up with all the baseball for all those years, and kept the family together.

> ...my only save seems like the only time that I ever got Tony Gwynn out.

Ironically, my only save seems like the only time that I ever got Tony Gwynn out. Everything about Tony was good.

WE WON'T BE BACK RIGHT AFTER THIS

KEITH OLBERMANN

On the night of October 17, 1998, he had already played seventeen Major League seasons. He had already won more batting titles than anybody except Ty Cobb and Honus Wagner. The last year he had not hit .300 was 1982.

By the night of October 17, he has already been to the World Series once and to the All Star Game fourteen times. He had already hit so well and for so long that when he shocked his admirers earlier that year with the first 0 for 15 hitless streak of his career, the Dodgers broadcaster, Ross Porter, calculated that he could extend that streak to 0 for 1,109 and still have a career average of .300.

He was about to bat .500 in his second World Series, about to hit a two-run homer in the first game, and then a two run single in the third game that gave his team its only lead of the Series, and with all that, Anthony Keith Gwynn was still nervous and excited.

"You're telling me I'm going to get to meet Bob Sheppard, THE Bob Sheppard. Oh man!"

As the 1998 World Series between Tony's Padres and the Yankees neared, he had said something about how much he was looking forward to finally getting to play at Yankee Stadium.

About how hearing the legendary public address announcer, Bob Sheppard, introduce him as he came to bat for the first time in Game 1, how that was going to be one of the thrills of his career. He was absolutely serious.

So, I took it a step further. I explained to Mr. Sheppard that the star of the Padres was a huge fan of his, and a huge fan of baseball history. The one man I had ever met in the game who seemed genuinely awestruck by people whose greatness or whose prominence he had far since eclipsed.

Bob said, "Take me to him." They talked, he and Bob Sheppard, as I remember it for ten or fifteen minutes. Tony Gwynn sprayed questions like he sprayed base hits. "Do you get nervous? What do you do to stay focused? I know you're a teacher. What do you try to convey to your kids?

I walked Mr. Sheppard back up to the press box and, en route, I asked him for another favor. And at some point after that all too brief Series ended, I heard from Tony Gwynn.

"You kidding me! How'd you do this?"

I had gotten Bob Sheppard to record the intro. "Now batting for San Diego, the right-fielder, number nineteen, Tony Gwynn, number nineteen."

I stuck the thing onto one of those talking photo-frame devices. I slipped in the photo of Tony with Bob and I sent it to Tony.

"It's in my trophy case," he giggled. "I put it next to my silver bats. If I keep pushing play I'm going to wear the thing out."

I told him I had another copy just in case. "But, wait a minute," I said. "You put it next to your silver bats."

"Yeah! What they give you for leading the League. This is the coolest thing. I even tried to say it along with him."

That was Tony Gwynn.

Was! He lived so much in the moment that it is impossible to think of him in the past tense. More than impossible. Almost cruel.

His statistics are extraordinary. He came to bat 10,232 times in the Majors. He **STRUCK OUT*** 4.2 percent of the time. He hit .338.

> *In 20 years in the big leagues, Gwynn **STRUCK OUT** only 434 times in over 10,000 plate appearances, roughly once a week. He had almost 800 walks in his career, averaging 1.8 walks for every strikeout, which is an amazing statistic. He walked more times than he struck out in each one of his Major League seasons except his rookie year, when he walked 14 times, but struck out 16 times in 54 games.

And without once clearing twenty homers in a season, he slugged .459. And he hit .300 every year for nineteen straight years from the time he was skinny and could also steal 56 bases in a season, till the time he wasn't and he couldn't.

But this isn't about his numbers. This is about him. You already know the story of Ted Williams and Tony Gwynn, of years of conversations between two San Diego guys who just happen to have the two highest career batting averages since 1939.

> I had to ask him to stop calling me 'Mister.'

It all culminated at the 1999 All Star Game in Boston when it was in part to see Tony Gwynn that Ted Williams even went to Fenway Park and created a baseball history moment to transcend all the others when he was engulfed by the present day stars and basically they would not let him leave the field.

I was the pregame host and the National League dugout reporter for the Fox broadcast of that All-Star Game, so when Tony Gwynn bounded back from the eternal lovefest, he found me.

"Did you see that." He had to give somebody a hug. It was me. "Did you see that? That was us with Ted Williams."

He didn't just treat the greats that way too. In Spring Training 1987, I was covering the Angels for my local station in Los Angeles. I have to say I was pretty good at it. But I could sit around the Gene Autry Hotel in Palm Springs, California, for hours at a time without anybody else knowing about it.

And one afternoon the Padres arrived, staying at the hotel. Came in on the 3:10 from Yuma or something, and stomped past the pool on their way to their rooms. And I saw Tony Gwynn, who, at that point, already had one of his batting championships, and one of his World Series trips, and three of his All Star Games. I saw him peel away from the crowd and walk towards me.

"Hi," he said tentatively. "Mr. Olbermann, my name is Tony

Gwynn. I play for the Padres. I watch you on Channel 5 every night. This is an honor."

I actually laughed. "I know you're kidding, Mr. Gwynn, but thanks."

He wasn't kidding. I had to ask him to stop calling me 'Mister.' Later, he would call me 'Mister' just to needle me.

You don't have to have had the privilege of knowing him to be heartbroken right now. What you hoped Tony Gwynn was like, he was like.

And I haven't even gotten into the charitable work, the health-awareness about smokeless tobacco and deep-vein thrombosis, the fact that he stayed in San Diego when the bigger stages beckoned. I doubt anybody in baseball history ever handed out more respect. Or—and this is an odd thing in sports—I doubt anybody in baseball history ever handed out more reassurance.

When he hit that batting slump in the summer of 1998, I did a piece on him for *Sports Illustrated* about giving out reassurance. I want to read just the end of the piece.

'When I saw Gwynn in the dugout at **DODGER STADIUM***, he was holding a small metallic device in one hand, so I asked him about the hamstring he had aggravated reaching for Cal Ripken's double in the All-Star Game. I pointed at the machine and asked, "Is that your electric stimulator? Is that your stim?" Gwynn laughed hard. "No, man. That's my mini-CD player. Will you relax?"'

What I would not give to have him reassure me that I'm overreacting right now. What all of us who knew or just knew of him would not give to hear him laugh right now and say "Will you relax?"

---

*When **DODGER STADIUM** opened in 1962, the Dodgers intended to have weekly boxing matches. They had only one because Davey Moore died after being hit by Sugar Ramos in the very first fight.

UMPIRE STATE OF MIND

KERWIN DANLEY

Kerwin Danley was a hard-hitting teammate of Tony Gwynn's at San Diego State. Disappointed at not being drafted, he turned to umpiring as his ticket to the majors. He made it to the Big Leagues in 1992 and was umping the game that Tony Gwynn collected hit number 3,000.

Tony never bragged about anything. He was the nicest man I ever knew. He wasn't ostentatious. That was just not his way. He played the game hard every day. He did it professionally, and at the end of the day he went home to his family.

Tony was just a good man. I don't know what else to even say about him. He was just a great man and I'm sure everybody else says that. I don't know why everyone who has great talent can't live their life like he did. He was always smiling. He was always joking and laughing. Nobody laughs like he did.

I remember one day during spring training, I ejected a player over something and Tony called me over. He said, "Kerwin, Kerwin, come on man. You know better. You're from Compton. I want to see that other side of you." It was like he was my coach.

The first game I umpired that Tony was playing in was in Atlanta and it was also my first game as a Major League Baseball umpire. What are the odds of that? The Padres were playing the Braves. Tony wished me good luck and told me that he knew I could make it as a big league umpire. He said, "You're a good guy, you've got a great background, and you'll be a good umpire." It's hard. Because I played with so many guys that I've grown up with. Growing up I've played on teams with Eric Davis, Darryl Strawberry, and Chris Brown. I played college ball with Al Newman, Tony Gwynn and Bobby Meacham. It's difficult to umpire your really good friends. You have to separate yourself from your friends in this game. I would never socialize with my baseball player friends during the season. It was just too hard. In the off-season it's a different story, I knew them before I got in this game.

I was umpiring the game in **MONTREAL*** when Tony got his 3,000th hit. That game wasn't even on my radar but as Tony got closer to his 3,000th hit, it was on TV all the time. As his friend, I was happy and hoping for the best for him. I looked at my schedule that month to see what cities I was going to umpire. I saw I was going to be in Montreal. A lot of times I don't know what team is going to be there. I just know I'm going to be in Montreal, and another team is going to be there. It doesn't matter what team it is, and I don't care what the standings are.

When I got to Montreal I looked at the schedule and I realized that the Padres were going to be there. I still didn't think I was going to be anywhere near when Tony got the hit. I didn't know what base I was going to be umpiring. Then, on the day of the game, I realized I was going to be at first and I thought, "Gee, he could get that hit today." Well, he ended up getting his 3,000th hit that day and I was at first base. It was very weird because I didn't know what to do when he got the hit. I really wasn't standing next to him and I wasn't going to go and shake his hand or anything like that. They called timeout. Then, Tony

*The night of Gwynn's 3,000th hit at Olympic Stadium in **MONTRÉAL**, attendance was announced at 13,540, but many tickets were bought over the phone or on the Internet by fans only interested in acquiring a souvenir of the historic night. Even fans at the game bought extra tickets, that started at $7 Canadian.

looked at me and he started coming towards me. I'm thinking, "What do I do?" Well, at that point it was all done. I was his friend and I was happy for him, so I shook his hand, gave him a hug, and congratulated him. I wasn't going to run away from him. I don't think it hurt the game any.

Tony was a great player. It was hard sitting back there calling strikes on him but he was so good. He knew the strike zone so well. The funny thing I remember is that his wife would get on me more than he would.

"Why are we taking all the good people from this world?"

Umpiring baseball has been a great experience and I wouldn't change anything for the world. I love the game of baseball and the game has been very good to me. I'm very proud of the fact that I kept at it and didn't let this game go. On our team at San Diego State, we all went to the major leagues in some way. We had Bobby Meacham, Bud Black, Al Newman, Tony Gwynn, as players; Steve Sayles as a trainer, and myself. Tell me what other school has that. Just one school, San Diego State. That is it....

When I got to college, all the guys dipped. One of the guys gave me Copenhagen. I remember it like it was yesterday. I got so sick I had to crawl back to my room. I have to laugh about it. That was literally not for me. Dipping tobacco was not for me.

It was tough when I heard that Tony had passed away. It was almost the same feeling I had when my dad had passed away. Tony was just such a great human being, as was my dad. It was almost a feeling of, "Why are we taking all the good people from this world?" There are some times when it's hard to swallow. It really is. I was really sad, really sad. I still am.

SOMETIMES GOD JUST HANDS YOU ONE

JOHN BOGGS

John Boggs is the founder, president, and CEO of JBA sports, an athlete representation and sports marketing agency that focuses exclusively on Major League Baseball. A graduate of American University, Boggs has counseled and represented many of the top players in baseball including Tony Gwynn, Alan Trammell, Paul Molitor, Cole Hamels, and Adrian Gonzalez in their contract negotiations and/or marketing endeavors.

I met Tony when his locker was right next to Steve Garvey's. At that time I headed up the Garvey Marketing Group. We struck up a relationship and started to do marketing projects together. Ultimately Tony and Alicia came into my office and asked if I would represent them because they were looking to make a change from their former agent. Alicia and Tony came to my office and Tony said, "I want you to be my guy."

I was so naive at that point, I didn't realize that here I had a guy who was the National League **BATTING CHAMPION***. All the brethren in my profession probably had a "hit" out on me— who the heck is this guy Boggs, he's got Tony Gwynn. Tony and I had a unique relationship, because he entrusted me with his career. I really hadn't been a practicing agent. I got certified and started representing him and doing his contracts. By the

---

*Tony Gwynn is the only Major League baseball player to win four **BATTING TITLES** in two different decades. Gwynn and Ty Cobb are the only players to have two separate strings of three or more consecutive batting titles. Gwynn had three in a row from '87 to '89, and then four in a row from '93 to '97.

time we were through we were more than just agent-player, we were really best friends.

He had a very strong compass and it was something that I was the beneficiary of. I think he realized my feelings towards him, because he was a very infectious person. Tony would never say "no" to an appearance or a marketing deal. His reaction was always appreciation for it. It made me want to go out and just get the next deal, and the next deal, and the next deal. That's the way he was, really genuine, the kind of person you just wanted to be around, and you felt blessed to be around. Then my being a baseball fan to be able to watch this incredible artist do his thing on the field from a ringside seat and really get to know the person was wonderful.

There were so many things that I learned over the years with Tony. First of all, people say that he was a hitting machine, but you know it took work, and that work took a lot of hours and a lot of sacrifice. I mean, heck, he'd go to the ballpark at 12 o'clock for a night home game. He lived there. He'd do his drills, his batting practice, and follow his routine. Then he would go out and get a hit. People thought he could just roll out of bed and go out there and get hits. No. It was work. He didn't like it when people said that he was a hitting machine, that he flipped the switch and started to hit, because he knew there was work involved. On his statue there is a quote from his father that says, "If you work hard, good things will happen." That's what he did.

He was a great defensive outfielder, but he worked on that harder than you could ever imagine. Not any one of his batting titles meant more to him than the first Gold Glove that he won. I was so privileged to be able to deliver that news to him. He was in Tennessee and he was sick in bed. But when I called and told him that news he was jumping up and down on the bed. He was so excited. He loved when he would work hard at something and get it done. If you told Tony he couldn't do something, he'd be the best at it before long, because he'd work at it.

He had the hand-eye coordination. He had the mechanics. But what Tony worked at was hitting the ball where it was pitched and reacting to certain pitches. He was probably a naturally gifted hitter, but he worked at being a great hitter. Some people will take that natural ability and just ride with it because it comes easy. Tony worked at it. It was a labor of love. He worked at it and worked at it, and worked at it.

It was so interesting to see him gravitate towards Ted Williams and have a talk about hitting. It was like watching two great minds coming together to discuss the craft that they were known for. One of the moments that stands out in my mind more than anything else in the world was when Ted Williams honored Tony at his Hitters Hall of Fame Museum in Florida. Tony wasn't the kind of guy who got into award ceremonies or pomp and circumstance or anything like that. He couldn't stand that. But I told him that he had to go. That was a little selfish on my part because I also wanted to go and see Ted Williams and be part of the award situation where Tony was going to be honored. On the final day, as we were leaving, Tony was in a hurry to go to the airport. After the ceremony Ted was having a luncheon and I said, "Tony, we've got to go to this luncheon." Tony reluctantly said, "Alright." I was glad he acquiesced, because he would have been more than happy to go to the airport.

We were sitting there at the luncheon and almost ready to leave, when Bob Costas' producer came over and said, "Would Tony mind sitting down with Bob and Ted for an interview?" They made this little area that was like a closet or a very small room for the interview. As we walked in, the **FIRST PRESIDENT BUSH*** was being interviewed with Ted and Bob, so we sat in the room and waited until that broke and President Bush left. Then it was Bob Costas, Tony, and Ted Williams. I will tell you

---

***PRESIDENT GEORGE H. W. BUSH** played first base for Yale in the 1947 College World Series in Kalamazoo, Michigan. The College World Series later moved to Wichita, Kansas before settling long-term in Omaha.

this, it was like an educational session and I was so happy I was not Tony Gwynn at that point in time. Because Ted, with his booming voice and personality, would bark out a question to Tony. I just sat there thinking, "Tony, please answer it right, please answer it right," because it was done in such a forceful way. He would ask, "What are you looking for on a 1-2 pitch?" Tony would answer it correctly and Ted would respond with, "Correct." And I silently would be going, "Yes."

In that interview, they covered every aspect of the game. Ted said, "What are you doing? You gotta hit more home runs." That's when Tony started to hit more home runs. He was still the gap-to-gap guy. He liked to kid himself and Rod Carew and Ozzie Smith that they were Punch and Judy hitters, but it was something Tony took away with him from that interview. Every aspect of hitting was discussed at that time. We left that luncheon, drove to Orlando for a plane and flew to San Diego. That's all that Tony and I talked about from the time we left all the way back to San Diego. It was an incredible moment. I like to say that I got to be a fly on the wall watching two great hitters discuss the art of hitting. It was unbelievable. It was fantastic. Tony just ate that up.

I can't say enough about Tony. He was so funny and so great to be around. He is just somebody I miss every single day. He was such a constant in my life, too. I talked to him every day...when he was not playing it might have been every other day. Or he'd come by the office on his way to San Diego State. He'd stop in three or four times a week. I still wait for that door to open up.

Tony had a great rapport with writers. He knew they had a job to do just like he had a job to do, and he let them do their jobs. From that, I think he got a lot of the benefit of the doubt, because writers respected him. He was sharp and he would catch them on things that weren't correct, or if they weren't prepared...or if a story had a lot of half-truths in it. It was interesting to watch him, and watch the writers around him.

Tony Gwynn changed my life. My only regret is that I couldn't say more to him before he passed away. He probably would roll his eyes because he just didn't want to hear that. He didn't like to be thanked or praised, or patted on the back. It wasn't important to him. I wear a National League championship ring that he gave me after the '98 Padres season. I was sitting in my house, it was about 11:30 at night. All of a sudden there was a knock at the door and it was Tony. He said, "Here. I thought you'd like this. And don't thank me." He dropped this ring in my hand. I said, "Tony, you've got to be kidding me." That was Tony.

Tony had been battling cancer for about three years. He'd had it removed. I noticed it at the **ALL-STAR GAME*** when they were doing this commercial for Pepsi. I told him that it looked like his cheek was swollen. He said, "Yeah, it's that cyst." I said, "It's back again? That's three times, Tony." He said, "It's nothing. It's benign." I told him he needed to have that looked into. Then later, I got the news from Alicia that Tony had cancer. Then it was the chemo, and then it was the radiation, and he battled through that. He came out of that and what happened was they went back again and realized it hadn't grown but it was still there on the nerves. They went in a second time and it was a radical surgery. That was the toughest because after that they did clinical trials. The clinical trials were not working well because it was painful going through his veins, sometimes it would work and sometimes it wouldn't work.

His health struggle captures the true essence of who Tony was—a grinder. He went through some difficult and painful times really grinning and bearing it. There were times he came into this office and I knew he was hurting but he would just chuckle and say, "I'll be alright." That's just what he did. It became very clear how much he accomplished after he had

***Gwynn started 11 ALL-STAR GAMES as a National League outfielder, the most ever in the National League.**

passed away when I looked closer at his record and I realized, "Wow, he accomplished a lot." The East Coast media didn't even know there was a team in San Diego for the most part. If Tony Gwynn had played on the East Coast in a major city, he'd be **DEREK JETER**[*] times 20 because of his consistency, and his loyalty too.

That guy wasn't going anywhere. He was a Padre. He loved San Diego. He was a throwback to the years that I used to love when you knew the lineups of every team, because they didn't change that often. You had a feeling of camaraderie towards the players. You could quote who was on the Big Red Machine, and when a trade came, it was a big deal.

He was from Long Beach but went to college in San Diego. He loved it, it was home. He felt very comfortable here and when you feel that kind of comfort and consistency you're crazy if you don't find a way or craft a way with the money that you're making to be happy. That's why he never left San Diego. It's really funny. They criticized Mike Trout for signing for $144 million and his response was, "Are you out of your mind? I like playing for the Angels. They're the organization I came up with. I enjoy playing here." How much money do you need?

Tony never went after it with that approach. He went after it with the approach of, "Where's home? What's best for my wife and kids? Do I like it? I'm a Padre." He used to be so proud to say, "I'm a Padre." That's why there's a street named after him here, there's a stadium named after him, and a statue in right field.

I had called Tony on Father's Day. I knew it wasn't good because Alicia told me to talk real loud and she would hold the phone to his ear. I had been with him two days before that and he was

---

[*]**DEREK JETER** was named after Derek Sanderson, former National Hockey League star with the Boston Bruins. Jeter's middle name is Sanderson.

not really responsive. He would just stare at you, so when she said that she'd hold the phone to his ear, I told him, "Hey I love you, buddy. Happy Father's Day. I hope you're feeling better and just try to keep everything positive." I hung up, and turned to my wife and said, "Wow, that can't be good. He can't hold the phone to his ear." Then at 1:20 a.m. that next morning, I got a call from Alicia. She was hysterical and told me that Tony had passed away.

I drove to the house at about 1:35 in the morning and stayed there until about 8 o'clock the next evening—just providing the support that I could. So many people did not know how sick he was.

Tony put value into people. Every-day people that he crossed paths with. When you meet people like Tony you get strength from them. It gives you more confidence that there are good people out there in the world and they're doing it the right way. That's another thing Tony said, "I just want to be known as somebody who did things the right way."

> Tony said, "I just want to be known as somebody who did things the right way."

He had an excellent upbringing by his parents. His brothers, Chris and Charles, are both great guys too. His mom and dad were great people. When Tony's dad passed away that put a heavy burden on him. Tony was an internal guy, he didn't wear things on his sleeve. He would internalize a lot of stuff that bothered him. He did have a great upbringing. He came from good stock, he really did. His parents taught all three sons how to do and go about things the right way.

The simple rules are the most direct and are the best guiding light that you can have. It's not complicated. It gets complicated when you're trying to maneuver around doing things the wrong way.

Any player who chews or dips needs to pay attention to this. The toughest part about this is that you look at guys who still dip and it's, "Hey do you want to get cancer? Do you want to get salivary cancer? Do you know what you're doing? You're playing the odds. It's incredibly crazy what you're doing." I don't know if it's just the ignorance of youth. But people are so image-conscious that if they see a big leaguer do it they're going to do the same thing. They think it looks cool, that it looks great when they're spitting it out. It's not that at all. It's absolutely crazy. That's why so many of these athletes say they're not role models, but yeah, they are, whether they like it or not, because people are going to imitate exactly what they do. When you're doing things that aren't good for you, they're going to imitate those things just as much. So you do have a responsibility. You've got to have an ounce of maturity to understand that what you do does affect people, whether you think it does or not. You have to take personal responsibility to realize that your actions do affect other people. A lot of people don't care.

Tony and Alicia took care of so many kids it was unbelievable. They took in people that were friends of friends or family. Some kids need mentoring and that house was always full. It was full of kids or people that they would want to give a better life to. It was inspiring. They were a giving family. That's the way they were in the community. That's the way they were in the family, that's the way they were with people they knew. If you needed some help Tony would do his best to try and help you. There will never be another Tony Gwynn!

BAT MAN

CHUCK SCHUPP

In 2014, Chuck Schupp retired after 35 years with Hillerich & Bradsby, the makers of Louisville Sluggers. He was the key liaison for Hillerich & Bradsby to all of their Major League Baseball clients. Schupp grew up in Louisville, attended the University of Louisville on a baseball scholarship, and played several years in the Minnesota Twins minor league system.

Back when Tony started playing there were five bat companies; now there are 28. My first purpose would be to find out if a player was happy, if there's something we need to do that we're not doing for the player. I would ask, "What do you look for in the bat that you want?" A lot of players would give you different answers on that, so it would be a professional conversation.

The more you do this, year after year, friendships develop. Just like in life, you gravitate towards certain players. Over the years that just happens, and Tony was one of those guys because he was always pleasant. He never made it like work for me to talk to him.

Tony used ash, and he liked wide grain which is basically the cross rings of the tree. Aesthetically, it's a good-looking piece of wood. He liked balance, because he never used a large bat lengthwise. He used 33-inch bats most of his career.

He always would laughingly say, "If I hit a home run, I didn't mean to hit a home run. I never try to hit a home run. It just happened." He was big on controlling the bat. He didn't care if it was excessively long or not. He knew the strike zone well enough that he just wanted a small bat that he could control.

But Tony also knew that if he wasn't hitting well it had nothing to do with the bat. It had to do with the hitter, so he would study his video, find out what he was doing wrong, and what he needed to do different or better. But why he sometimes would change bats? A lot of guys would use the phrase, "I'm just going back to what I'm comfortable with." Players don't give you specifics sometimes, just the 'feel'. When somebody says, "It feels right," it's hard to quantify what that means.

He was usually a 32-ounce guy. Sometimes he might tweak it a half an ounce here and there. Guys do that sometimes late in the season, just because they're tired and they'd want a little bit lighter bat. Tony, more than any hitters I've ever dealt with, was very **CONSISTENT*** with what he ordered, so we basically reloaded what he ordered, and went from there.

Tony was easy to be around. As a person he was low maintenance. He didn't ask for a whole lot. He just wanted to be consistent, and that's a pretty fair thing to ask for. From time to time, Alicia would do some collectible projects and we would work with her. John Boggs, Tony's agent, is one of my closest friends in the business. I knew John when he worked with Steve Garvey, prior to Tony Gwynn.

I've also worked with Tony's brother Chris, and his son Anthony Jr. I knew Chris about as well as Tony. As you know, Tony had a very distinctive voice and laugh. Without even looking in the clubhouse when Tony would talk or laugh, you knew it was him. His son has exactly the same voice as Tony. It's eerie. When I first met him I thought, "Man, he sounds exactly like his father." Like Tony, both Chris and Anthony Jr. were very polite.

---

*In the 14 seasons from 1984 to 1997, Gwynn finished in the top five in the batting race 13 times. In the only season he didn't, 1990, he missed by one hit.

They knew they were there to do their job, and they appreciated you helping them.

It's a very competitive business. When you Google officially licensed Major League bats, you're going to get a laundry list of companies you've never even heard of before. I'm sure other companies tried to talk to Tony, would approach him and ask if there was anything they could do for him. That's the nature of the business. Tony never wavered, and there's not many guys you can say that about over their entire career. Derek Jeter is one of the customers that I had. He never swung another product, and I know there are people that talked to him. After a while, once those guys have enough tenure, if you have any respect for the game or what they're doing, you leave them alone.

> There's an old wives' tale that you should hold the bat with the trademark up.

There's an old wives' tale that you should hold the bat with the trademark up. If the bat is made of maple it doesn't matter as much, but with ash it really does because the brand is on the weak side of the bat, so you're making contact with the strongest side of the wood. Whether you're holding the bat facing you or facing 180 degrees away from you it doesn't matter. But if you turn that bat a quarter turn, it can increase exponentially the chance that bat is going to crack or break.

In terms of percentage of total bat usage it's more maple than ash, because the maple just lasts longer. It's harder to break, so the teams get more at-bats for their dollar. Right now, it's about 70% maple, 30% ash. Louisville Slugger makes both. Tony Gwynn used ash bats.

Tony used aluminum bats in college. When the aluminum bat first came out, it had its benefits. There were cost savings. The performance was out of whack, 'cause the things were so "hot," it just skewed the game. With the rule changes in college, the aluminum bats they use now have been dialed way back performance-wise. It's to the point now that the game has changed to the opposite direction. They're also going to change the balls in college baseball next year to actually add more offense to the game.

Our Silver Slugger Award presentation always occurs the spring after the player wins the batting title. It's an on-the-field presentation. It seemed like every April I was flying to San Diego to present the award to Tony. With a guy who was that pleasant to be around, I was excited every year to do it because it was fun. He was always excited to receive that award. The reception the fans would give him in San Diego was awesome because the guy was loved there.

Everybody always asks me, "Who's the nicest guy you met in baseball?" You meet and talk to so many players over 30 seasons, just outstanding human beings. Tony is without a doubt in the top five players I've ever met. It's hard to put one above another but you've got Tony, you've got guys like Ozzie Smith, Jim Thome, Craig Biggio—there are just so many guys that were good people who played the game the way it's supposed to be played.

I hope that players who hear about Tony, or talk about him, or look at the way he played his career would take some guidance from that, and use it to make them better players. He worked very hard, he was a student of the game, but he was also very polite and gracious. There was not a "look at me" type of attitude in him. I know that's probably hard to ask for, because in this day and age things are talked about for 72 hours, and then we move onto the next news story. Guys like Tony have impacted me in as far as how you treat people and how you succeed in life. He succeeded in life, and it's very sad that he's not going to be with us a lot longer than he was. I tell players I wish they would have been able to meet Tony Gwynn because he just did things the right way.

BAT WOMAN

CHARLOTTE JONES

Charlotte Jones is retired after a long career working for the Louisville Slugger company. She forged a close friendship with Tony Gwynn, her most unforgettable player ever.

I loved my job at Louisville Slugger, and I was very, very lucky to get it. I had worked for Nabisco at a local warehouse here in Louisville for Oreos, Fig Newtons, and Ritz Crackers. I went to a temporary agency. They sent me to Hillerich and Bradsby—the Louisville Slugger people—to type. I told the lady at the agency that I couldn't type. She said, "Well just go on down there and fake it." So I took my little dictionary and my spell-check book with me, and for three months I was a temporary person. Then, a job came open.

They had a big layoff in '81 and the layoff was not only in the factory, but also in the office. It got right up to me. I was divorced at the time, raising three children, and going to school. I like to think that they appreciated me and my work ethic. So, for two years I floated. When my boss, Chuck Schupp, or his predecessor, Rex Bradley, were out of the office, I would go in and answer the phone for them and work in the pro bat department. And then, the next week, maybe someone would be out in the **GOLF*** department, or someone would be out in the sporting goods department, so for two years they let me

*While playing **GOLF** in 1567, Mary, Queen of Scots, was informed that her husband, Lord Darnley, had been murdered. She finished the round.

float from department to department. Then, in 1984, they said, "Okay, you're going to sit here, and take pro bat orders every day." Of course, over the next 29 years, there were times when I had to also do athletic goods orders and the golf orders. We used to have a hockey division, also. I never did hockey orders, they were all done in Canada.

I was the girl in high school that didn't like history. So it was ironic to have my livelihood, my income to be so dependent upon the history of baseball. In the sixth grade, my teacher was a nun. She played softball with the boys every day. Now we're talking back in the '60s, but the girls had to play volleyball. Every October, she would close the curtains to the classroom and we would watch the World Series in sixth, seventh, and eighth grades.

One of my little young cousins one time wanted to go to a movie, and I said no, we're going to a baseball game. He didn't want to go to the baseball game. I just told him that the movie will be there tomorrow, that movie will be the same. But each game, every day something different is going to happen.

I am an only child, I don't have any brothers, but I do remember my father listening to baseball games on the television or the radio. I actually grew up about six blocks from the old Louisville Slugger factory in Louisville, Kentucky. As a child, I used to see the billets of timber as they transported them down the street.

The timber arrived in round billets. There are usually 276 pieces in a stack, and then they have these little railroad cars with metal wheels, and each wagon would hold one of these stacks. They would pull these little cars through the streets of Louisville with a tractor.

Tony Gwynn was a great person. He was baseball. My boss for 29 years was Chuck Shupp. He was the guy that went into the clubhouses and went to spring training. I sat behind the computer screen, and processed the orders. We always had a rule that Chuck talked to all the players and agents, and I would talk to the equipment managers and all the old-timers....the retirees like Willie McCovey and Willie Mays who had the time to call in and talk. But of course, whenever Chuck was on the road or at spring training, then I would field these calls.

Many different players would call in, and one particular time Tony was searching. He was looking for something. Brian Prilaman, the Padres equipment manager, called me. Brian was trying to tell me over the phone how he wanted us to adjust the bat for Tony. "Shave a little bit off the handle six inches up, a little bit off the barrel," and Tony finally said, "Give me the phone. Let me talk to her."

Tony told me over the phone how he wanted the model adjusted for his feel. Then I transported the information to the bat makers. The majority of the time Tony used a thirty-two and a half inch bat. Very short. Most of the players were using thirty-four or thirty-five inch bats. Typically, at that time in the

> He had a bat one time that he called the "Seven Grains of Pain."

'80s, we didn't even make anything any smaller than thirty-three inches for major league players or even minor league players.

All of these players would get a hold of Tony's bat, and they'd want to have something like Tony Gwynn used. I would have to tell them, I'd say, "Yeah, but Tony Gwynn is a batting champion. You're not going to get what Tony Gwynn gets."

He had a bat one time that he called the "Seven Grains of Pain." He used that bat for one year. He would hit with it and he would take it back and lock it up. Then, first day of spring training he did crack it. They said he literally just had tears in his eyes because this bat had finally broken. I'm not sure why he called it the 'seven grains of pain,' but in my mind I think it was because of the grains in the bat, and because of all the pain he caused to the opposing team whenever he came up with that bat.

Any time I would go to Cincinnati, of course being a woman, I did not impose upon the clubhouse. I was delivering bats. I was there to speak to Prilaman about his needs, the orders for the players, and any complaints the players had. Tony would always come in the back room. It was always, "Miss Charlotte, how are you doing?" He'd walk right out of the batting cage, and be sweaty, and he'd apologize for being sweaty. And I'd say, "Tony, that's fine. Just give me a hug." I don't even know that I have an autograph from him in my possession, but just those memories of him taking the time, coming in the back room, just, "How are you doing? How's the family?" And me back at him, "How' Alicia? How's your son? Your daughter?"

Even after he retired, he'd call up and say he needed a couple of dozen bats. Then it was Coach Gwynn. He'd call up and ask "How are you doing? How's the family?"

Some players would call up all full of themselves and say, "This is Mr. so-and-so." And I'm supposed to snap to it because they're calling Louisville Slugger. But with players like Don **MATTINGLY*** and Tony Gwynn it was always very personable. Great guys to work with and it made my job even more enjoyable.

One of my other fondest memories was in the late '80s, early '90s, I had family that lived in California. We went to a game one night in San Diego, but I did not get there early enough to see Brian or any of the players before the game. After the game, Brian got me down to an anteroom away from the clubhouse. I particularly asked if Tony was busy. This was an hour or an hour and a half after the game. You could hear noise

---

*Don Mattingly hit six grand slams in 1987, an all-time Major League record for one season. **MATTINGLY** never hit a grand slam before or after that season.

in a batting cage: pitching, slamming, and so on. Brian said that Tony was doing his workout. This is what he did after the game. I was unable to see him that night, but you just really got the feel of the guy, his routine, and his love of the game. He'd already been in the game eight or nine years, and here was Tony Gwynn still doing batting practice after the game was over.

I believe it was two years ago that he came to Louisville. Louisville Slugger has a Living Legends Award each November. He and Alicia came together to accept the award. His love of his wife, his love of his family.... When you say Hall of Fame, there's a reason those guys are in the Hall of Fame. It's a certain personality and quality of man. I am going back to guys like Pee Wee Reese and the older guys, Brooks Robinson and some of the really greats in the game.

When he came to Louisville in 2012, he already had had the surgeries on his face. He looked good, and he looked healthy at that time, but it just made you wonder where he was going.

Tony would have to be at the top of all the players I worked with just because my tenure ran at the same time as he got called up in '81. In 1984, the Padres were in the World Series, and that year was my first year full-time doing pro bat orders. I probably shouldn't say that, because I worked with so many of the older guys—**YOGI BERRA***, Willie McCovey, Harmon Killebrew, and the ones today—Cal Ripken Jr., and Ozzie Smith and just so many of them, I can't name all of them, but just the love of his family, the dedication to baseball set Tony Gwynn right up there at the top for me.

I do miss talking to the older guys, the customers, and all the different teams. I was taught that you should not show any

---

*A young Martha Stewart was the Berra family babysitter when **YOGI** played for the Yankees.

partiality, because all 30 teams were buying bats from us, but my first year, '84, was with the Padres and the Tigers in the World Series, so I do follow the Padres and the Tigers. I was also fortunate to work a couple of years with Pee Wee Reese, so I've got a little Dodger Blue in me, and then again we're only ninety miles from the Cincinnati Reds. They were very very good to me over the years when I delivered bats to them. My customers were more than just customers, I was on the phone with them daily, taking their orders, checking their orders, processing the orders, and I do miss talking to the different players.

Some of my favorite players, in no particular order, were Harmon Killebrew, Brooks Robinson, Yogi Berra, Steve Garvey, Willie McCovey, Paul O'Neill, and Ken Griffey Jr.

I could always tell what city Ken Griffey Jr. had been in because the next day some equipment manager or some player would be calling wanting to "get bats just like Junior uses." That's used to be the joke, you know, "whatever Junior was using."

Terry Francona. When I used to go to Cincinnati, and my car would pull up with the bats, Terry Francona would come out and help unload the **BATS*** out of my car. I don't know whether he wanted to see who was getting bats and what everybody was getting, but if he was in that back room or if they said the lady from Louisville Slugger was here, it just seemed that he was always there ready to unload the bats, which was a clubhouse kid's duty. Dave Parker—he was a personality, he was a hoot.

My boss Chuck Shupp let me take the Silver Slugger to Tony Gwynn one April. Silver Sluggers are awarded each year to the batting champ in each league. Rather than packing it up and shipping it, I flew into San Diego with the award. This was

---

*Orlando Cepeda used more **BATS** than any player in baseball history. He felt each bat had exactly one hit in it. When Cepeda hit safely, he would discard the bat. He had 2,364 hits in his career.

before 9/11. When I got on the plane, I told the stewardess that I had this metal bat with me. She looked at me kind of funny and said, "I'm going to have to talk to the pilots about that."

They said that the only way I could get on the plane with the metal Silver Slugger bat was if it could ride in the cabin with the pilots, and if they could open it up, look at it, touch it, and hold it. They needed to be sure that it was going to the San Diego Padres to be presented to Tony Gwynn. The box was 36-inches long and it would probably have been difficult to get it in an overhead cabin bin anyway.

The pilots were amazed when they opened the box, took out the beautiful Silver Slugger award, and knew that it would be going from their hands to his. The bat rode in the cabin with the pilots all the way from St. Louis to San Diego.

> **They needed to be sure that it was going to the San Diego Padres to be presented to Tony Gwynn.**

It was the Silver Slugger award. It had a copy of Tony's signature on the bat, and exactly what he had hit that year to win the batting title. I don't know if that was when they were pure silver or if it was silver polished. It is an amazing award, and Tony got eight of them in his career.

When we lose someone or we have hard times, people say, "Why did God do this to me?"...I was taught God put us on earth with a choice. We can go either this way or we can go that way. Tony Gwynn was definitely a man who made the choice to live his life a certain way. As he traveled through this life he made a lot of us happier and he entertained so many of us by the way he played the game. He wanted to be a part of the game.

He just wanted to be part of the game. That was his choice. That's the way he played, day in and day out. He was just admirable (sobbing). He was just a good guy.

BAT BOY

DAVID JOHNSON

David Johnson was born in San Diego in 1974, spent the 1991 season as a bat boy for the San Diego Padres, went to college in Minnesota, and has been slowly drifting back West ever since. He currently divides his time between Portland and Eugene, Oregon, where he toils in the salt mines of academia.

The baseball-card collection I had as a teen—145,000 cards in all when I last bothered to count, 800-count box after 800-count box, all of them occupying a dusty bookcase in my bedroom—was sold years ago. Some random stranger now owns that collection of 400 Tom Glavine rookie cards I bought on speculation at $.04 each. (I haven't checked Beckett recently, but I'm sure that investment has more than doubled.) The tiny handful of cards I kept each serve a purpose. Some remind me that people are idiots (Bill Ripken's card); some remind me that we all start somewhere (Ken Griffey Jr.'s San Bernardino Spirit card), and others remind me, as if I need reminding, that Tony Gwynn was one of the finest human beings I've ever met, and that the world is cheaper without him in it.

Most 10 year-old boys walk through life searching for a hero. I found mine in the form of a chubby singles hitter from San Diego State University. I began to actively idolize Tony Gwynn in 1984, the year the unassuming team in Mission Valley put together something magical and made lifelong fans of a collection of people who mostly thought of the ballpark as somewhere to hang out on Sunday afternoon if you were tired of the beach.

I wasn't alone in my worship among my friends, but I tried to do it best. Most of my friends had a Tony Gwynn poster on their walls—I had at least eight. Tony Gwynn growth charts. Tony

Gwynn sliding into home. Tony Gwynn in a "Hitting Machine" poster, done up in the style of architectural renderings to capture the mechanics of his swing. Newspaper clippings covered my door. Shirts, mugs, hats, you name it—all bore Tony's face. I would mentally recite Tony's biography to myself each night instead of counting sheep. ("Anthony Keith Gwynn was born on May 9, 1960. His parents were Charles and Vendella Gwynn. He had two brothers, Charles and Chris ...").

These were the late 1980s. Back then, a kid's illusions about his sports heroes were much harder to shatter. There was no social media to lift the veil and let you see the plain truth. Talk radio was fairly sanitary, especially in sleepy little San Diego. The local newspaper may have had harsh words, but those were reserved for upper management—the players, especially Tony, were granted a decorous exemption. So my idolatry continued unchecked. I collected Tony's cards and had a few chance encounters with him over the years, like the time I was introduced to him by my neighbor's ex-husband who happened to be his college roommate. (I told you San Diego was a sleepy little town in those days.) I continued to recite his bio, which I updated to include each passing season, the birth of his kids, his stats, to get myself to sleep. "Tony's son, Anthony Gwynn Jr., was born on ..."

> I was 13. "Write back when you're 16," they replied. I did...I got an interview.

In 1988, I wrote a letter to the San Diego Padres, saying I wanted to be a bat boy. I was 13. "Write back when you're 16," they replied. I did, and, miraculously, I got an interview. Utterly lacking the connections that land most bat boys the job, I put together a "résumé" (work experience: mowing lawns; education: 3.67 GPA through 11th grade), letters of reference (from a soccer coach, my fifth-/sixth-grade teacher, and my science teacher), and a personal statement. Somehow, I got the job. My first day of work was March 31, 1991, and I was tasked with unloading the team truck, freshly arrived from spring training in Yuma, Ariz. I spent seven hours that night hauling huge boxes out of a semi truck. I drove home covered in sweat and moths. I loved every minute.

My title was "Bat Boy, San Diego Padres." It was a primo job for a 16-/17-year-old. Free parking pass! Free tickets to every game! Free team ID card! Seats in the dugout for half the game, seats down the foul lines for the other half! None of that mattered—leading up to the season, the only thing I knew was that I was going to be working alongside Tony Gwynn. We were going to be co-workers! If any teammates tried to cut him down, like the treasonous Jack Clark had years before, I'd stand up in the locker room and defend him! We'd become friends! These are the thoughts of a 16-year-old kid about to work within spitting distance of his hero.

> Have you noticed that the tributes to Gwynn all seem to mention his laugh?

You know where this story ends for most kids. They idolize a figure they know from afar, they get an improbable chance to meet the guy, and he turns out to be a bum. He cheats on his wife. He kicks over trash cans. He shouts at clubhouse attendants. My first day at the stadium, I stood getting dressed in my sparkling new uniform in the bat-boy locker area, which was tucked around a corner from the main locker room, and located about 10 feet from the bathroom. Players filed by, most of them ignoring us. Suddenly, he appeared.

"Hey," he said to me, holding out his hand. "I'm Tony. How are you?" Flustered, I stammered, "Uh, nothing much." He laughed.

He laughed! Have you noticed that the tributes to Gwynn all seem to mention his laugh? The man's laughter illuminated the room. "Best sound I've ever heard in my life," ESPN's Chris Berman said in the locker room one day, after I'd sheepishly hauled out my Chris Berman baseball card and asked for his autograph. Somebody—my memory says it was Bruce Hurst—said, "I know that's your rookie card, Chris, 'cause you've got hair in that photo." Tony laughed for the next five minutes straight, literally holding his sides he was laughing so hard. The joke was lame, but who cares? If the payoff is hearing Tony Gwynn laugh for five minutes, I'll sit through anything.

One day, one of the bat boys showed up wearing an earring. Bright gold and massive. The Giants were in town. During batting practice, Will Clark walked by and sneered, "Nice earring, faggot." The words were stunning, but we knew we had to react like it was no big thing. News must've gotten around, though, because before the next game, Tony walked back to the locker room area with Bip Roberts and performed an entire routine for us. They had evidently practiced it during batting practice. They stood lecturing us, using every "how to talk like an older white guy" cliché in the book. "Now listen, son," Tony started, stopping periodically to catch his breath, as he was laughing too hard. "You're bringing down the team here, with that earring." "Very, very unprofessional," Bip added, haughtily. They walked away, howling with laughter, the point made: **WILL CLARK*** was a jerk.

Before one game, early in the season, I stood out in right field during batting practice, arms folded. Tony walked over. "Want to toss?" he asked. Trembling with nervousness, I said, "Yeah," and tried to act like this was nothing to me. My first toss went about 30 feet over his head. He laughed and ran after it. Second toss, only 15 feet over his head. He jogged over to me. "How are you holding that ball?" he asked. I showed him my grip. "Well heck, that's all wrong." A 10-second lesson, and we were good to go. He fired a rocket to me. I fielded it cleanly and threw it back using my new grip. This time only five feet overhead. He

---

*Tony Gwynn needed a hit in his last at bat of the 1989 season to edge out **WILL CLARK** for the batting title. Gwynn singled.

laughed again, harder this time. I got myself under control, and we threw for 10 minutes, just us. At one point I stopped, realizing that some kids were watching. They were watching me. They were watching me playing catch with Tony Gwynn. I could read their thoughts: "That kid is so lucky." I was. On my way back to the clubhouse, one of the kids, some poor 6-year-old totally overcome by the moment, asked me for my autograph. I signed his program. Tony watched. He laughed the whole time.

I wonder what it must be like to know that you have a destabilizing effect on people. Some people use this knowledge to their own benefit. The Padres' catcher that season, Benito Santiago, was a renowned curmudgeon—that's a polite way to say he was a complete and unrepentant --------—and he relished his bad reputation. "You can tell the manager that he may ---- --------- ---," he told me one day when I brought around a dozen baseballs the manager wanted signed for a charity auction. "Um," I told the manager, "Benito was busy."

Tony went the other way—he knew he had a profound effect on us, and he embraced it. He talked to us. He asked us about classes. He asked us if we were dating anybody. (Hey, Tony, I never told you this, but that girl I told you about, the one I said I really liked but who didn't like me back? We've been married for 12 years. We've got two kids. You were right.)

The last home stand of the season, Tony's official Nike catalog showed up in our locker one day, with a note in his familiar handwriting. "Pick a pair," the note said. We each happily circled a pair with the pen he provided. Later that week, before a game, the shoes appeared in our locker, along with a check for $500 for each of us. I didn't even care about the money itself— THIS WAS A HANDWRITTEN CHECK FROM TONY GWYNN. PAYABLE TO ME. (I think I waited five months to cash that check. When I did, the bank teller's eyes got big and she looked down at the check, up at me, down at the check.) A few games after the shoes appeared, the equipment manager, our boss, told us: "You know, Tony drove down to Foot Locker himself and bought those shoes for you guys. You probably thought he had them delivered or something. But he went down there. That's what he does."

When kids have heroes, they tend to build them up into something unsustainable, something doomed to crumble, and years later, as adults, they look back on the their old enthusiasms with gentle condescension. On Monday, June 16, 2014, I turned on my computer and the words "Hall of Famer Tony Gwynn dies at 54" hit me square in the chest. I lost my breath for a minute. In that instant, dozens, hundreds of memories of Tony flashed through my mind. And each one remains good, clean, and perfect in its own way.

> ...dozens, hundreds of memories of Tony flashed through my mind. And each one remains good, clean, and perfect in its own way.

Here's one: I was 12 or 13, hanging out near the player's parking lot after the game, waiting for autographs. Tony was the big "get," and I sat there for a good three hours after the game. Suddenly, he appeared. He looked so normal, wearing jeans and a polo shirt. He walked over to his truck, a 4x4 with PADRE19 as the license plate. "Tony! Tony!" I and a few other die-hards shouted. He walked over cheerfully and signed stuff we could fit through the fence. He signed my baseball card and handed it back to me. "Tony," I said. "Thank you." He looked right back at me: "You're welcome." That killed me. It still kills me. It was the simplest gesture; it was the kindest.

DO YOU WANT MORE TONY GWYNN?
AN ADDITIONAL BONUS CHAPTER FREE!
SAME FORMAT

GO TO: WWW.GOSTEALTHISBOOK.COM/TONYGWYNN

TO BE CONTINUED!

We hope that you have enjoyed *Tony Gwynn: He Left His Heart in San Diego.* Due to space and time considerations many great stories could not be included. They will be included in a book *For San Diego Sports Fans Only.*

If you have a neat Tony Gwynn, San Diego Chargers, San Diego Padres, or San Diego Clippers story, contact us today by email at printedpage@cox.net. Pay attention to this next line... we might have a pop quiz later. Please put the story title and your phone number in the subject line...or just call the author directly at 602-738-5889. He'll probably answer...he's a lonely old man with no friends and a lotta time on his hands.

Your story could be in the new book.

Note: No actual Los Angeles Dodgers fans were harmed in the making of this book.

Other Books by Rich Wolfe

For Cardinals Fans Only—Volume I
For Cardinals Fans Only—Volume 2
Remembering Jack Buck
I Remember Harry Caray
Ron Santo, A Perfect 10
Jeremy Lin, The Asian Sensation
For Cubs Fans Only
For Cubs Fans Only—Volume II
For Notre Dame Fans Only—
    The New Saturday Bible
Da Coach (Mike Ditka)
Tim Russert, We Heartily Knew Ye
For Packers Fans Only
For Hawkeye Fans Only
I Love It, I Love It, I Love It (with Jim Zabel, Iowa announcer)
Oh, What a Knight (Bobby Knight)
There's No Expiration Date on Dreams (Tom Brady)
He Graduated Life with Honors and No Regrets (Pat Tillman)
Take This Job and Love It (Jon Gruden)
Remembering Harry Kalas
Been There, Shoulda Done That (John Daly)
And the Last Shall Be First (Kurt Warner)
Sports Fans Who Made Headlines
Fandemonium
Remembering Dale Earnhardt
I Saw It On the Radio (Vin Scully)
The Real McCoy (Al McCoy, Phoenix Suns announcer)
Personal Foul (With Tim Donaghy, former NBA referee)

For Yankee Fans Only	*For South Carolina Fans Only*
For Red Sox Fans Only	*For Clemson Fans Only*
For Browns Fans Only	*For Oklahoma Fans Only*
For Mets Fans Only	*For Yankee Fans Only—Volume II*
For Bronco Fans Only	*For Mizzou Fans Only*
For Michigan Fans Only	*For Kansas City Chiefs Fans Only*
For Milwaukee Braves Fans Only	*For K-State Fans Only*
For Nebraska Fans Only	*For KU Fans Only (Kansas)*
For Buckeye Fans Only	*For Phillies Fans Only*
For Georgia Fans Only	

All books are the same size, format and price.
Questions or to order? Contact the author directly at 602-738-5889.